Weight Watchers®
Slim Ways™
GRILLING

Weight Watchers®
Slim Ways™
GRILLING

Macmillan • USA

Golden barbecue forks to everyone who helped put this cookbook together: recipe developers Gloria Bakst, Amanda Cushman, Luli Gray, Tamara Holt, Toni Oppenheimer, Diane Schwalb and Donna Shields, M.S., R.D.; copyeditors Allison Cleary, Deri Reed, Eileen Runyan and Evie Righter Talbot; nutrition consultants Lynne S. Hill, M.S., R.D., L.D., and William A. Hill, M.S., R.D., L.D.

Editor-in-Chief: Lee Haiken
Food Editor: Joyce Hendley
Book Editor: Martha Schueneman

Cover photo by Martin Jacobs

MACMILLAN

A Simon & Schuster Macmillan Company
1633 Broadway
New York, NY 10019-6785

Library of Congress Cataloging-in-Publication Data

Weight Watchers slim ways : grilling
        p.   cm.
    Includes index.
    ISBN 0–02–861007–5 (alk. paper)
    1. Reduce diets—Recipes.   2. Barbeque cookery.   I. Weight
Watchers International.
    RM222.2W3274   1996
    641.5'63—dc20   95–49104
                            CIP
Manufactured in the United States of America
10 9 8 7 6 5 4 3 2 1

WEIGHT WATCHERS

Since 1963, Weight Watchers has grown from a handful of members to a leading name in safe, sensible weight control. Today millions enjoy our popular, expanding line of convenience foods, best-selling cookbooks, audio and video tapes and weight-loss management products.

For best weight-loss results, we recommend that you attend Weight Watchers meetings, follow the Weight Watchers food plan and participate in a regular program of physical activity. For the Weight Watchers meeting nearest you, call 1-800-651-6000.

CONTENTS

INTRODUCTION

FIRE UP THE GRILL!

All of us have memories of something wonderful we've had cooked outdoors, whether it's the first time we tasted a grilled hot dog at a grade-school picnic, or an unforgettable grilled ear of corn on a camping trip. Indeed, fire, heat and the great outdoors all seem to conspire to make grilled food taste so good. Grilling also imparts wonderful flavors without adding fat and calories, making it one of the leanest cooking methods around.

You don't need to be an expert chef to be a terrific grill cook. All you need is good weather and some great recipes—like the ones you'll find here. You'll learn the basic techniques of grilling like a pro—from selecting the right grill to marinating foods perfectly. Then, you're ready to move on to barbecue greatness!

GETTING STARTED: A GRILL ROUND-UP

There's a grill to suit nearly everyone's taste and budget, and each has its fans. Deciding which grill is best for you depends on the kind of grilling you do most often, and for how many people you'll be cooking. Here are the main types from which to choose.

OPEN GRILLS

These simple models, such as the popular hibachi or bra-
zier types, are usually the least expensive. With shallow
bottoms that hold a smaller amount of coals, they are best
for quick-cooking items that lie flat, such as steaks, chops and
kabobs, although some models may come with attachments
for spit-roasting. They have the advantage of being
portable, making them ideal for picnics and camping.

COVERED GRILLS

This is the most popular grill type, and with good rea-
son: It can perform double-duty as an open grill (cover
off) or a closed one (cover on). When closed, the grill allows
hot, smoky air to circulate around the food, functioning
somewhat like an oven. The result: Food cooks faster, with
less turning, and picks up a smokier flavor. Popular types
include the covered kettle barbecue, in the familiar
"clamshell" shape, or box-shaped grills with hinged lids.

GAS GRILLS

For those who prefer not to use charcoal, a gas grill is the
solution. Ceramic briquets or lava rocks are heated by gas
jets, and they radiate heat quickly—the grill can be ready in
as little as 10 minutes. Gas grills have covers that allow for
both open and closed grilling. They are fueled either by
a refillable propane gas unit or through a permanent con-
nection to a natural gas line. Some charcoal enthusiasts
swear that gas-grilled foods don't taste as smoky as char-
coal-grilled ones, but most gas-grill aficionados disagree.

INDOOR GRILLS

If it's raining—or if you'd like to barbecue in the dead of winter—an indoor
grill can come close to re-creating the taste of the great outdoors. You'll find
several types on the market, including small electric units (some with built-in

rotisseries) or special grill surfaces that rest directly on top of a gas or electric stove. One of our favorites is a cast-iron grill pan with a raised-ridge surface, which acts like a grill rack.

EQUIPMENT EXTRAS

All you really need for a barbecue is a grill, some way to heat it, something with which to turn the food, such as a long-handled spatula or tongs, and extra-long oven mitts to protect your hands. If you're a serious griller, however, you'll soon find the gadgets below to be indispensable; stock up over the course of the summer until you have everything you need. Most are available in the barbecue section of hardware or home stores and in some supermarkets.

CHARCOAL CHIMNEY STARTER

A charcoal chimney starter is a cylindrical metal container with a handle that allows you to get charcoal going quickly without using lighter fluid, making it an environmentally smart choice. Stack the briquets into the top level and fill the bottom level with crumpled newspaper. Light the newspaper with a match and the coals will be ready in about 12 minutes. Simply turn out the hot coals directly into the grill.

ELECTRIC FIRE STARTER

The electric fire starter is a metal loop that you place in a bed of coals and plug in. It usually lights the coals within 10–15 minutes.

GAS IGNITER

This gun-shaped gas lighter with a long barrel allows you to spark prepared charcoal quickly and safely.

GRILL BASKET

This rectangular basket fits over a grill, with small perforations or tightly spaced grids that allow you to grill smaller items, such as shellfish and vegetables, which might otherwise fall through the spaces in the grill rack. Some are shaped like woks, enabling you to stir-fry on the grill.

MEAT THERMOMETER

Hands down, the meat thermometer is the quickest, most accurate way to judge doneness!

LONG-HANDLED TONGS

Great for turning and moving coals as they cook, long-handled tongs prevent you from burning your hands.

LONG-HANDLED BASTING BRUSH

This brush is for basting foods with marinade or barbecue sauce as they grill.

WIRE BRUSH

Essential for clean-ups, the wire brush has bristles that scrape accumulated residue off the grill after cooking. It can easily be cleaned with hot soapy water.

THE FUEL

CHARCOAL BRIQUETS

Briquets are the most common choices for grilling and are widely available. Quick-lighting briquets contain chemical starter; they can be lit just with a match (do *not* use starter fluid). Since the chemical starter can quickly dissipate into the air, light the coals immediately after placing them in grill, and always keep the bag tightly closed. Lump-charcoal chunks are easier to light, but they can burn unevenly due to their irregular shapes.

WOOD CHIPS OR CHUNKS

With a few handfuls of wood chips or chunks and a closed grill that allows smoke to surround the food, you can add a smoky, complex flavor to food you're grilling. Simply choose the wood with the flavorings you prefer; mix together two or three types, if you like. The most popular woods include mesquite, which adds a woodsy flavor that is ideal for southwestern cooking, and hickory, with its sweet, mellow Southern-style flavor. Apple- or cherrywood add sweet smokiness to fruits and mild-flavored meats and poultry; delicate-flavored alderwood is the traditional choice for smoking fish.

If you're grilling something for a brief time—say, cut-up chicken or fish—choose wood chips. Long-burning wood chunks are best for longer-grilled items. Soak them in water for at least 30 minutes, then toss them onto the hot coals. In a gas grill, the soaked wood pieces can be placed in a foil pan with a little water added; the pan can then be put directly on the lava rocks or ceramic briquets.

PREPARING THE GRILL

If you have a gas grill, simply follow the manufacturer's instructions for lighting and preheating the grill. For charcoal grills, start first with the right amount of coals. Use 12–25 briquets for a short-burning fire—enough to cook steaks, chops and burgers. For a longer-burning fire lasting more than 30 minutes, or for large items like roasts, start with 30–40 briquets and add more coals as needed.

Remove the grill rack and pile the coals into a pyramid in the center of the barbecue; use starter fluid or an electric or chimney starter and light. The coals are ready when they are covered with white ash, in about 40–45 minutes.

COOKING METHODS: DIRECT OR INDIRECT

When the coals are ready, they can be arranged for two different methods of cooking: direct or indirect. In the direct method, coals are spread out in the middle of the grill and the food is cooked directly above. This method cooks food quickly, resulting in more browning on the outside of the food. Direct cooking is best suited for smaller pieces of food such as kabobs, steaks, chops, burgers or vegetables.

With the indirect method—an option only with covered grills—the heat surrounds the food rather than radiating directly onto it. It's the preferred method for cooking larger, thicker items such as whole roasts or other large cuts of meat. The food is placed directly over a drip pan—a foil or foil-covered heat-resistant pan that is slightly larger than the food being grilled. (A foil pie pan makes a great drip pan.) The hot coals are then spread around the drip pan, and the lid is closed. In gas grills with two burners, one burner is lit and the food is placed directly above the other, unlit burner.

CONTROLLING THE HEAT

Most grills allow you to adjust the temperature of your fire in some way. At the very least, you can raise or lower the grill rack—higher for longer, slower cooking, and lower for quicker, hotter cooking. Opening the side vents and letting in more air will cause the coals to burn faster and get hotter; closing them halfway will slow the fire; and closing them completely will extinguish it. Here are some other ways to get the temperature you want, once the coals have been heated:

LOW FIRE

Spread out coals, leaving $1/2$" space between them, removing some coals if necessary. Close vents halfway.

MEDIUM FIRE

Spread out coals so that they are still touching, in a double layer.

HOT FIRE

Tap ashes off hot coals with tongs, and move coals closer together; add a few more coals to fill (*do not use starter fluid*). Open vents fully.

IS IT HOT ENOUGH YET?

Some barbecues come with temperature gauges, and you can find barbecue surface thermometers in hardware stores. There's also an easy way to gauge temperature with your hand. Simply place your hand, palm-side-down, eight inches directly above the hot coals. Keep your hand there until the heat feels uncomfortable, counting the seconds. Use the following as a guide:

If you can hold your hand over the fire:	The temperature is:
5 seconds	Low
4 seconds	Medium
3 seconds	Medium-Hot
2 seconds	Hot

NOW YOU'RE COOKING

When the coals are almost ready, it's time to replace the grill rack: *Before placing it on the grill,* spray the grill rack evenly with nonstick cooking spray, then place it on the grill's medium level, about 5" from coals (unless otherwise directed). *Do not* spray the grill rack while it is on the grill; a dangerous flare-up could result.

Allow the prepared grill rack to heat up at least 5 minutes on the grill before placing food on the grill; foods tend to stick to a cold grill rack.

MARINATING KNOW-HOW

Many of the items in this book are marinated before they are placed on the grill—to boost their flavor and, in the case of some meats and poultry, to tenderize them. As all good grill chefs know, the right marinade can turn a tough cut of lean meat or a mild-flavored vegetable into something juicy and wonderful. Marinades also add richness and flavor impact—with little if any fat—so they can be a blessing when you're trying to eat more healthfully.

The key elements in a marinade are herbs, spices and other aromatic ingredients for flavoring, and acidic ingredients such as wine, vinegar, lemon juice or yogurt for tenderizing. Some oil may be added to impart a little juiciness or to keep foods from sticking to the grill. See "Marinades, Sauces and Make-aheads" (page 143) for delicious marinade ideas.

BARBECUE SAFETY SMARTS

• Begin with a clean grill; clean the grill grid with a wire brush and empty the ash-catcher. (A full ash-catcher can prevent air from getting to the coals.)

• Trim as much fat as possible from meats and poultry; fat dripping on the grill can cause flare-ups.

• Keep the barbecue away from anything flammable, including dry grass, hanging tree limbs, the garage or any volatile materials.

• Do not use kerosene or gasoline to light coals; use only starter fluid —and *never* add starter fluid to quick-lighting briquets or hot coals.

• Never start a gas grill with the lid shut.

• Keep a spray bottle full of water handy to quench any flare-ups.

• Never leave a hot grill unattended, especially around children.

• Don't leave the coals burning when you have finished grilling; douse them in water and stir until the fire is completely out.

• Store propane cylinders upright, away from children. Keep out of sunlight or enclosed areas.

We prefer marinating foods in sealable plastic bags for several reasons. First, the plastic bags do not react with the food or marinade and thus do not impart any flavors of their own to the food; second, they are compact and fit easily into a crowded refrigerator. And, last, they're convenient—no dishes to wash! If you don't have sealable plastic bags, use a glass, plastic or ceramic bowl or dish to marinate foods; cover tightly with plastic wrap and refrigerate.

Here's the smart way to marinate food:

1. In appropriately sized sealable plastic bag (large enough to contain the food item or items), shake or swirl marinade ingredients to combine.

2. Add food; seal bag, squeezing out air. Turn bag over to coat food.

3. Place in refrigerator for specified length of time, turning occasionally. Larger cuts of meat will take longer to marinate, often overnight; fish and small pieces of poultry can take as little as 10 minutes.

Other marinade musts include the following:

1. Always marinate meat, poultry and fish in the refrigerator. Do not let them stand more than 30 minutes at room temperature before grilling.

2. If you are going to use a fish, meat or poultry marinade as a sauce, the marinade must be fully cooked before using to avoid bacterial contamination. Drain off marinade into a saucepan and bring to a rolling boil; let boil at least one minute, stirring constantly. Remove from heat, let cool to room temperature and refrigerate if not using immediately.

1

APPETIZERS AND SOUPS

Grilled Bagel Chips • Tomato Bruschetta • Wild Mushroom Bruschetta
Garlic Cheese Bread • Spicy Tomato Salsa • Pineapple Salsa
Roasted Eggplant "Caviar" • Grilled Zucchini–White Bean Dip
Raita • Grilled Vegetable Kabobs with Lemon Scallion Dipping Sauce
Grilled Corn Chowder • Grilled Mushroom Soup • Grilled Beet Borscht
Grilled Gazpacho • Cold Grilled Peach–Melon Soup

GRILLED BAGEL CHIPS

You can flavor these versatile chips with any combination of dried herbs and spices. They go beautifully with Grilled Zucchini–White Bean Dip (page 9).

Makes 4 servings

One 4-ounce bagel, halved
    and sliced lengthwise into
    16 chips
1 teaspoon vegetable oil

Pinch salt
Pinch garlic powder
Pinch dried oregano

1. Prepare grill for a medium fire, using direct method (see page xiii).
2. Grill bagel chips, 2–3 minutes, turning once, until golden brown.
3. In shallow plate, toss chips with oil and seasonings until well coated. Transfer to serving bowl and serve.

Serving (4 chips) provides: $1/4$ Fat, 1 Bread.

Per serving: 88 Calories, 2 g Total Fat, 0 g Saturated Fat, 0 mg Cholesterol, 184 mg Sodium, 15 g Total Carbohydrate, 1 g Dietary Fiber, 3 g Protein, 22 mg Calcium.

TOMATO BRUSCHETTA

Bruschetta (broo-SHEH-tah) comes from an Italian word meaning "to roast over coals." The classic version uses only juicy, ripe tomatoes and fresh, plump garlic.

Makes 4 servings

Four 2-ounce slices (1" thick)
   large round coarse French or
   Italian bread
1 large garlic clove, halved

2 large ripe tomatoes, cut
   into 8 slices each
4 fresh basil or mint leaves, slivered
2 teaspoons fruity olive oil

1. Prepare grill for a medium fire, using direct method (see page xiii).
2. Toast bread slices on edges of grill, just long enough to crisp and char lightly; turn and toast other sides.
3. Immediately rub with garlic halves; wrap loosely in foil and keep warm.
4. In small bowl, gently toss tomatoes with basil and olive oil; arrange on bread slices and serve immediately.

Serving (1 slice) provides: ¹/₂ Fat, 1¹/₂ Vegetables, 2 Breads.

Per serving: 202 Calories, 4 g Total Fat, 1 g Saturated Fat, 0 mg Cholesterol, 356 mg Sodium, 35 g Total Carbohydrate, 3 g Dietary Fiber, 6 g Protein, 54 mg Calcium.

WILD MUSHROOM BRUSCHETTA

This meaty-tasting dish makes a flavorsome appetizer for a meal of grilled vegetables, or a fine side dish with grilled poultry. If you are using shiitake mushrooms, it's wise to use a grill basket so that you don't lose any to the coals.

Makes 4 servings

Four 2-ounce slices (1" thick)
  large round coarse French or
  Italian bread
1 large garlic clove, halved
4 portobello or 12 shiitake
  mushrooms (8 ounces),
  stems removed

2 teaspoons olive oil
$^1/_4$ cup minced shallots
$^1/_4$ cup low-sodium chicken broth
1 tablespoon balsamic vinegar
Freshly ground black pepper,
  to taste

1. Prepare grill for a medium fire, using direct method (see page xiii).
2. Toast bread slices on edges of grill, just long enough to crisp and char lightly; turn and toast other sides.
3. Rub bread with garlic halves; wrap loosely in foil and keep warm.
4. Grill mushrooms on edges of grill, just long enough to char lightly. Wrap in foil to steam and keep warm.
5. Place small skillet over medium heat or at edge of grill 30 seconds. Add oil; heat 30 seconds more. Add shallots; cook, stirring constantly, just until wilted, about 2 minutes. Add broth, vinegar and pepper; bring to a boil. Reduce heat and simmer, uncovered, 1 minute. Stir in mushroom juices that have accumulated in foil.
6. Slice mushrooms and arrange on bread slices. Drizzle evenly with oil mixture and serve.

Serving (1 slice) provides: $^1/_2$ Fat, 1 Vegetable, 2 Breads, 1 Optional Calorie.

Per serving: 197 Calories, 4 g Total Fat, 1 g Saturated Fat, 0 mg Cholesterol, 356 mg Sodium, 34 g Total Carbohydrate, 2 g Dietary Fiber, 6 g Protein, 51 mg Calcium.

GARLIC CHEESE BREAD

This garlicky cheese bread is so decadent! It is great for company, and kids will love it, too. If you are not a garlic fan, use just a touch, or omit the garlic entirely.

Makes 4 servings

1 1/2 ounces shredded part-skim
    mozzarella cheese
3/4 ounce freshly grated
    Parmesan cheese
1/2 cup minced fresh basil

4–6 medium garlic cloves, minced
1/4 teaspoon freshly ground
    black pepper
4 ounces French bread, halved
    horizontally

1. Preheat grill for a medium fire, using direct method (see page xiii).
2. In small bowl, combine mozzarella and Parmesan cheeses, basil, garlic and pepper; toss well. Sprinkle cheese mixture over cut sides of bread; with fingers, press firmly onto bread. Close the bread, sandwich style; wrap in heavy-duty aluminum foil.
3. Grill bread, turning once, until hot and cheese is melted, 8–10 minutes. Remove foil and cut bread into 8 slices. Serve immediately.

Serving (two 1/2-ounce slices) provides: 3/4 Protein, 1 Bread.

Per serving: 122 Calories, 3 g Total Fat, 1 g Saturated Fat, 4 mg Cholesterol, 273 mg Sodium, 19 g Total Carbohydrate, 1 g Dietary Fiber, 5 g Protein, 146 mg Calcium.

SPICY TOMATO SALSA

This classic salsa is a delightful accompaniment to any grilled meat, chicken or fish—or serve it with fresh-cut veggies or pita wedges toasted on the grill. Be sure to use ripe tomatoes, as they provide most of the flavor.

Makes 4 servings

1 1/2 cups seeded diced tomatoes
3/4 cup diced onions
2 tablespoons minced
   fresh cilantro
1 tablespoon minced jalapeño
   pepper (wear gloves to
   prevent irritation)

2 teaspoons white vinegar
2 medium garlic cloves, minced
1/4 teaspoon salt

In medium nonreactive bowl, combine tomatoes, onions, cilantro, jalapeño pepper, vinegar, garlic and salt; stir well. Cover and set aside at least one hour to blend flavors before serving.

Serving (1/2 **cup**) **provides:** 1 Vegetable.

Per serving: 28 Calories, 0 g Total Fat, 0 g Saturated Fat, 0 mg Cholesterol, 143 mg Sodium, 6 g Total Carbohydrate, 1 g Dietary Fiber, 1 g Protein, 13 mg Calcium.

PINEAPPLE SALSA

The sweet and sour flavors of this tropical salsa complement grilled chicken or pork.

Makes 4 servings

³/₄ cup (6 ounces) diced
   Grilled Pineapple (page 168)
3 tablespoons coarsely chopped
   red onion
¹/₂ teaspoon chili powder
1 medium garlic clove,
   finely minced

¹/₈ teaspoon salt
Pinch ground red pepper or
   dash hot red pepper sauce
¹/₂ teaspoon cider vinegar
   (optional)

In medium nonreactive bowl, combine pineapple, onion, chili powder, garlic, salt and pepper. Depending on sweetness of pineapple, add vinegar to taste. Cover and refrigerate until ready to use.

Serving (¹/₄ cup) provides: ¹/₄ Fruit, 20 Optional Calories.

Per serving: 39 Calories, 0 g Total Fat, 0 g Saturated Fat, 0 mg Cholesterol, 24 mg Sodium, 10 g Total Carbohydrate, 1 g Dietary Fiber, 0 g Protein, 12 mg Calcium.

ROASTED EGGPLANT "CAVIAR"

This dip is nice as a centerpiece for a plate of cut-up vegetables, or it can be served with pita and vegetable chips.

Makes 4 servings

1 medium eggplant
2 tablespoons minced fresh parsley
2 tablespoons fresh lemon juice
1 tablespoon minced onion
1 garlic clove

$^1/_4$ teaspoon salt
$^1/_8$ teaspoon freshly ground black pepper
2 medium Belgian endives (8 ounces), leaves separated

1. Prepare grill for a low fire, using direct method (see page xiii).
2. Slice eggplant in half lengthwise; with paring knife gently cut $^1/_2$" cross hatch pattern through flesh, being careful not to pierce skin.
3. Place eggplant halves skin-side down on coolest part of grill; grill 25 minutes, until soft and bubbling. Allow to cool slightly and scoop pulp from shells, avoiding any burned parts. Discard shells.
4. In blender or food processor, combine grilled eggplant, parsley, juice, onion, garlic, salt and pepper; purée until blended to the consistency of lumpy oatmeal.
5. Transfer dip to small serving bowl; cover and refrigerate if not serving at once. Place bowl on platter, surround with endive leaves and serve.

Serving ($^1/_4$ cup + $^1/_2$ cup endive leaves) provides: 2 Vegetables.

Per serving: 50 Calories, 0 g Total Fat, 0 g Saturated Fat, 0 mg Cholesterol, 147 mg Sodium, 12 g Total Carbohydrate, 4 g Dietary Fiber, 2 g Protein, 57 mg Calcium.

GRILLED ZUCCHINI–WHITE BEAN DIP

This tastes best at room temperature, and it goes well with Grilled Bagel Chips (page 2).

Makes 8 servings

1 medium zucchini, thinly sliced lengthwise
2 cups drained rinsed white kidney (cannellini) beans
2 tablespoons minced fresh parsley
1–2 tablespoons fresh lemon juice
1–2 garlic cloves, minced
2 teaspoons olive oil
1/2 teaspoon salt
1/4 teaspoon freshly ground black pepper

1. Prepare grill for a medium fire, using direct method (see page xiii).
2. Grill zucchini 5 minutes, turning once, until slightly charred and fork-tender.
3. In blender or food processor, combine zucchini, beans, parsley, juice, garlic, oil, salt and pepper; purée until smooth.
4. Transfer to a serving bowl; cover and refrigerate if not serving at once.

Serving (1/4 cup) provides: 1/4 Vegetable, 1 Protein.

Per serving: 64 Calories, 2 g Total Fat, 0 g Saturated Fat, 0 mg Cholesterol, 88 mg Sodium, 0 g Total Carbohydrate, 3 g Dietary Fiber, 4 g Protein, 21 mg Calcium.

RAITA

This Indian yogurt-based condiment, pronounced RAY-ta, makes a great starter for a summer barbecue meal. Instead of grilling, you can toast the pitas conventionally indoors.

Makes 4 servings

1/2 teaspoon cumin seeds
2 cups plain nonfat yogurt
2 medium cucumbers, pared, halved, seeded and grated
1/4 cup finely minced red onion

1 tablespoon + 1 teaspoon minced fresh mint
1/2 teaspoon salt
2 large (2-ounce) pitas, split

1. In small skillet over low heat, toast cumin seeds just until fragrant, about 2 minutes. Transfer to cutting board and crush seeds with mallet or flat side of large knife, or crush with mortar and pestle.
2. In small bowl, combine yogurt, cucumbers, onion, mint, salt and crushed cumin. Cover and refrigerate 1 hour.
3. Prepare grill for a medium-hot fire, using direct method (see page xiii).
4. Grill pita halves 1–2 minutes per side, until golden and crispy, being careful not to let them burn. Cut each pita half into 8 wedges.
5. Place bowl on platter, surrounded with pita wedges and serve.

Serving (1/2 cup raita with 8 pita wedges) provides: 1/2 Milk, 1 Vegetable, 1 Bread, 15 Optional Calories.

Per serving: 153 Calories, 1 g Total Fat, 0 g Saturated Fat, 2 mg Cholesterol, 516 mg Sodium, 27 g Total Carbohydrate, 1 g Dietary Fiber, 10 g Protein, 266 mg Calcium.

GRILLED VEGETABLE KABOBS WITH LEMON SCALLION DIPPING SAUCE

Serve these hot with grilled meats, cold or at room temperature as a salad. Vary the vegetables according to your preferences.

Makes 4 servings

1/2 cup chopped scallions
1/2 cup plain nonfat yogurt
1/2 teaspoon minced lemon zest*
2 tablespoons fresh lemon juice
1 teaspoon hot red pepper sauce
1/4 teaspoon salt
1/8 teaspoon freshly ground
   black pepper

1 medium zucchini, halved lengthwise and cut into 1" chunks
1 medium yellow squash, halved
   lengthwise and cut into
   1" chunks
2 cups mushrooms, quartered
18 cherry tomatoes
2 teaspoons vegetable oil

1. Prepare grill for a medium fire, using direct method (see page xiii). If using wooden skewers, soak in water 30 minutes.
2. In small bowl, combine scallions, yogurt, zest, juice, pepper sauce, salt and pepper; set aside.
3. Thread zucchini, squash, mushrooms and tomatoes onto eight 12" metal or wooden skewers, dividing evenly and alternating to create a colorful pattern; brush with oil.
4. Grill kabobs 10 minutes, turning once, until cooked through. Place 2 kabobs on each of 4 plates; serve 3 tablespoons sauce on the side.

Serving (2 kabobs with 3 tablespoons sauce) provides: 1/2 Fat, 3 Vegetables, 15 Optional Calories.

Per serving: 74 Calories, 3 g Total Fat, 0 g Saturated Fat, 1 mg Cholesterol, 199 mg Sodium, 10 g Total Carbohydrate, 2 g Dietary Fiber, 4 g Protein, 86 mg Calcium.

The zest of the lemon is the peel without any of the pith (white membrane). To remove zest from lemon, use a zester or vegetable peeler.

GRILLED CORN CHOWDER

This wonderful, comforting soup picks up added flavor from the roasted corn. Make it ahead—it's even better the next day.

Makes 4 servings

1 tablespoon + 1 teaspoon reduced-calorie tub margarine
1 medium yellow bell pepper, diced
1 medium onion, diced
$^1/_2$ cup diced celery
$^1/_4$ cup minced shallots
2 tablespoons all-purpose flour
1 cup low-sodium chicken broth
10-ounces all-purpose potatoes, pared and diced

$^1/_2$ teaspoon salt
$^1/_4$ teaspoon ground white pepper
$^1/_4$ teaspoon paprika
1 bay leaf
2 cups grilled corn kernels (page 162)
1 cup low-fat (1%) milk
1 cup evaporated skimmed milk
$^1/_2$ teaspoon hot red pepper sauce
2 tablespoons minced fresh chives

1. Place large saucepan over medium heat 30 seconds; melt margarine 30 seconds more. Add bell pepper, onion, celery and shallots and cook, stirring constantly, 10 minutes, until wilted. Add flour and cook, stirring constantly, 5 minutes. Stir in broth, potatoes, salt, pepper, paprika and bay leaf and simmer, covered, 20 minutes.
2. Add corn, milk, evaporated milk and pepper sauce; simmer 15 minutes more, but do not allow to boil.
3. Remove and discard bay leaf. Divide soup evenly among 4 bowls; garnish each with $1^1/_2$ teaspoons minced chives and serve.

Serving ($1^1/_2$ cups) provides: $^3/_4$ Milk, $^1/_2$ Fat, 1 Vegetable, $1^1/_2$ Breads, 20 Optional Calories.

Per serving: 283 Calories, 5 g Total Fat, 1 g Saturated Fat, 5 mg Cholesterol, 489 mg Sodium, 53 g Total Carbohydrate, 5 g Dietary Fiber, 13 g Protein, 293 mg Calcium.

GRILLED MUSHROOM SOUP

Grilled mushrooms give this light soup a full flavor.

Makes 4 servings

¹/₄ cup balsamic vinegar	2 teaspoons minced fresh thyme
1 tablespoon olive oil	leaves
2 large (4") portobello mushroom	1 teaspoon reduced-sodium
caps	soy sauce
8 ounces white mushrooms	¹/₄ cup minced fresh parsley
¹/₂ cup chopped onion	¹/₄ teaspoon salt
2 medium garlic cloves, minced	¹/₄ teaspoon freshly ground
1¹/₂ ounces long-grain white rice	black pepper

1. Prepare grill for a low fire, using direct method (see page xiii). Spray grill basket with nonstick cooking spray.
2. In medium bowl, combine balsamic vinegar and 1 teaspoon of the oil; add portobello and white mushrooms and toss well.
3. Grill mushrooms in prepared grill basket 15–20 minutes, turning once, until cooked through.
4. Meanwhile, place medium saucepan over medium heat 30 seconds; heat remaining 2 teaspoons oil 30 seconds more. Add onion and cook, stirring frequently, 4 minutes, until translucent. Add garlic and cook 1 minute more. Add 4 cups water, the rice, thyme and soy sauce. Bring to a boil, reduce heat and simmer 15 minutes, until rice is cooked.
5. In blender or food processor, combine mushrooms and 1 cup of the rice mixture; purée until finely chopped. Return to saucepan with rice mixture, stir and gently reheat to serving temperature. Stir in parsley, salt and pepper. Divide evenly among 4 bowls and serve.

Serving (1 cup) provides: ³/₄ Fat, 2 ¹/₄ Vegetables, ¹/₂ Bread, 10 Optional Calories.

Per serving: 103 Calories, 4 g Total Fat, 1 g Saturated Fat, 0 mg Cholesterol, 192 mg Sodium, 15 g Total Carbohydrate, 2 g Dietary Fiber, 3 g Protein, 23 mg Calcium.

GRILLED BEET BORSCHT

This traditional Russian soup picks up an intriguing new flavor from the grill. If you prefer, serve it hot.

Makes 4 servings

6 medium beets
2 cups low-sodium chicken broth
1 cup shredded cabbage
1 cup low-calorie cranberry
   juice cocktail

$^1/_2$ cup diced onion
1 tablespoon granulated sugar
1 teaspoon salt
$^1/_4$ cup nonfat sour cream
   (optional)

1. Prepare grill for a low fire, using direct method (see page xiii). Rinse beets and remove greens; save for another use.
2. Grill beets, turning occasionally, 35–45 minutes, until tender. Cool beets, peel and dice; there should be about 2 cups.
3. In medium saucepan, combine beets, broth, cabbage, juice cocktail, onion, sugar and salt; simmer over low heat, stirring frequently, 40 minutes.
4. Refrigerate, covered, 3–4 hours. Divide evenly among 4 bowls; garnish each with 1 tablespoon sour cream (if using), and serve.

Serving (1 cup without sour cream) provides: $^1/_4$ Fruit, $1^3/_4$ Vegetables, 30 Optional Calories.

Serving with sour cream: add 10 Optional Calories.

Per serving (with sour cream): 62 Calories, 1 g Total Fat, 0 g Saturated Fat, 0 mg Cholesterol, 638 mg Sodium, 13 g Total Carbohydrate, 1 g Dietary Fiber, 3 g Protein, 35 mg Calcium.

Per serving (without sour cream): 62 Calories, 1 g Total Fat, 0 g Saturated Fat, 0 mg Cholesterol, 648 mg Sodium, 14 g Total Carbohydrate, 1 g Dietary Fiber, 4 g Protein, 35 mg Calcium.

GRILLED GAZPACHO

Grilling the vegetables gives a smoky twist to this chilled soup.

Makes 4 servings

1 large red onion, quartered	$^1/_2$ teaspoon salt
1 large green bell pepper, quartered	$^1/_2$ teaspoon freshly ground
8 large plum tomatoes, halved	black pepper
3 garlic cloves, chopped	Hot red pepper sauce, to taste
2 tablespoons fresh lime juice	$^1/_2$ cup diced cucumber
1 tablespoon balsamic or red	
wine vinegar	

1. Prepare grill for a hot fire, using direct method (see page xiii).
2. Grill onion and bell pepper, 8–10 minutes, and tomatoes, 2–3 minutes, turning once, until slightly charred on all sides.
3. In blender or food processor, purée grilled onion, bell pepper and tomatoes with the garlic, juice, vinegar, salt and black pepper until smooth. Season to taste with pepper sauce; transfer to a nonreactive bowl, cover and refrigerate overnight.
4. Divide evenly among 4 bowls; and garnish each with 2 tablespoons of the diced cucumber and serve.

Serving (1 cup) provides: 3 $^3/_4$ Vegetables.

Per serving: 62 Calories, 1 g Total Fat, 0 g Saturated Fat, 0 mg Cholesterol, 291 mg Sodium, 14 g Total Carbohydrate, 3 g Dietary Fiber, 2 g Protein, 32 mg Calcium.

COLD GRILLED PEACH-MELON SOUP

This refreshing soup is a great way to begin a meal on a hot summer evening.

Makes 4 servings

4 medium peaches, pared, pitted and quartered	3 tablespoons fresh lemon juice
2 cups diced cantaloupe	1 tablespoon minced fresh mint leaves
1 cup fresh orange juice	4 whole mint leaves

1. Prepare grill for a medium-hot fire, using direct method (see page xiii). Spray grill basket with nonstick cooking spray.
2. Place peaches in basket in a single layer; grill 3 minutes per side.
3. In blender or food processor, combine grilled peaches, cantaloupe, orange and lemon juices and mint; purée until smooth. Transfer to a nonreactive bowl, cover and chill 3–4 hours.
4. Divide evenly among 4 bowls; garnish with whole mint and serve.

Serving (1 ¹/₄ cups) provides: 2 Fruits.

Per serving: 114 Calories, 0 g Total Fat, 0 g Saturated Fat, 0 mg Cholesterol, 8 mg Sodium, 28 g Total Carbohydrate, 3 g Dietary Fiber, 2 g Protein, 23 mg Calcium.

2

POULTRY

Grill-Roasted Chicken with Garlic-Rosemary Rub • Tarragon-Vanilla
Grill-Roasted Chicken

Lemon Chicken with Basil • Grilled Curried Chicken and Apples

Key West Jerk Chicken • Super-Quick Orange-Glazed Drumsticks

Gingered Chicken Kabobs • Chicken Burgers

Curried Chicken-Tofu Burgers with Mango-Peach Chutney

Grilled Turkey Burgers with Roasted Onion Topping • Tabbouleh Turkey Burgers

Grill-Roasted Whole Turkey Breast with Sage • Grilled Turkey Cutlets
with Cranberry-Orange Salsa

Grilled Cornish Hens with Raspberry Glaze • Cornish Hens with
Wild Mushroom Stuffing

Grilled Squabs • Grilled Quails • Tandoori Pheasant

Capon with Chocolate-Chipotle Sauce • Grill-Smoked Duck Breast
with Red Cabbage

GRILL-ROASTED CHICKEN WITH GARLIC-ROSEMARY RUB

This is undoubtedly the perfect way to cook chicken; try not to peek too much during the cooking!

Makes 6 servings

One 3-pound 6-ounce
  chicken
2 garlic cloves, minced
1 tablespoon minced fresh
  rosemary leaves or
  1 teaspoon dried, crumbled

2 teaspoons salt
1 teaspoon freshly ground
  black pepper
1 lemon, halved

1. Prepare grill for a medium fire, using indirect method (see page xiii).
2. Rinse chicken thoroughly inside and out; pat dry with paper towels. Discard giblets and remove visible fat. Rub inside and out with garlic, rosemary, salt and pepper. Squeeze lemon juice over chicken and place lemon halves in chicken cavity. Tuck wings under breast and truss.
3. Grill chicken, covered, with all grill vents open, 1 hour, until cooked through and juices run clear when thigh is pierced in thickest part with fork.
4. Cut chicken into 6 equal pieces; divide evenly among 6 plates and serve. Remove skin before eating.

Serving (3 ounces chicken) provides: 3 Proteins.

Per serving: 168 Calories, 6 g Total Fat, 2 g Saturated Fat, 76 mg Cholesterol, 808 mg Sodium, 3 g Total Carbohydrate, 0 g Dietary Fiber, 25 g Protein, 36 mg Calcium.

TARRAGON-VANILLA GRILL-ROASTED CHICKEN

You won't believe how juicy and flavorful this golden bird becomes on the grill. The combination of tarragon and vanilla is so subtle that no one will guess your secret ingredients.

Makes 8 servings

One 3-pound chicken
1 small garlic clove
6–8 fresh tarragon sprigs
$^1/_4$ teaspoon salt

$^1/_2$ teaspoon freshly ground
black pepper
$^1/_4$ cup low-sodium chicken broth
2 tablespoons vanilla extract

1. Prepare grill for a medium fire, using indirect method (see page xiii).
2. Rinse chicken thoroughly inside and out; pat dry with paper towels. Discard giblets and remove visible fat. Rub chicken cavity with garlic clove. With your fingers, gently loosen breast skin and insert a tarragon sprig under the skin of each breast. Stuff remaining sprigs in cavity; tuck wings under breast and truss. Rub chicken all over with salt and pepper.
3. To prepare basting sauce, in small bowl or cup, combine broth and vanilla.
4. Grill chicken, covered, with all grill vents open, 50–60 minutes, brushing every 10 minutes with basting sauce, until cooked through and juices run clear when thigh is pierced in thickest part with fork.
5. Cut chicken into 8 equal pieces; divide evenly among 8 plates and serve. Remove skin before eating.

Serving (2 ounces chicken) provides: 2 Proteins, 1 Optional Calorie.

Per serving: 121 Calories, 4 g Total Fat, 1 g Saturated Fat, 50 mg Cholesterol, 118 mg Sodium, 1 g Total Carbohydrate, 0 g Dietary Fiber, 16 g Protein, 10 mg Calcium.

LEMON CHICKEN WITH BASIL

This citrus-flavored dish can be made up to 12 hours ahead and stored, covered, in the refrigerator.

Makes 4 servings

1 teaspoon grated lemon zest*
3 tablespoons fresh lemon juice
1 tablespoon + 1 teaspoon
    vegetable oil
2 garlic cloves, minced
1 teaspoon minced pared
    fresh ginger root
15 ounces skinless boneless
    chicken breasts, cut into
    4 equal pieces

$^{1}/_{2}$ teaspoon salt
$^{1}/_{4}$ teaspoon freshly ground
    black pepper
1 large red bell pepper,
    cut into thin strips
2 tablespoons coarsely chopped
    fresh basil

1. Combine zest, juice, oil, garlic and ginger; add chicken and marinate at least 1 hour or overnight (see page xvi).
2. Prepare grill for a medium fire, using direct method (see page xiii); spray grill basket with nonstick cooking spray.
3. Remove chicken from marinade with tongs; drain marinade into small saucepan. Bring to a rolling boil; boil for one minute, stirring constantly. Remove from heat.
4. Season chicken with salt and black pepper and grill 8 minutes, turning once, basting with marinade, until cooked through. Grill pepper strips in grill basket about 6 minutes, until slightly charred.
5. To serve, place one piece of chicken on each of 4 plates, scattering one-fourth of pepper strips over and around each. Sprinkle each with one-fourth of the basil.

Serving (3 ounces chicken, with $^{1}/_{4}$ of pepper strips) provides: 1 Fat, 1 Vegetable, 3 Proteins.

Per serving: 200 Calories, 8 g Total Fat, 1 g Saturated Fat, 72 mg Cholesterol, 338 mg Sodium, 5 g Total Carbohydrate, 1 g Dietary Fiber, 27 g Protein, 35 mg Calcium.

---

*The zest of the lemon is the peel without any of the pith (white membrane). To remove zest from lemon, use a zester or vegetable peeler. To grate zest, use a zester or fine side of a vegetable grater.

GRILLED CURRIED CHICKEN AND APPLES

Curry subtly flavors both the chicken and apples here. Increase the amount of curry powder if you'd like a more intense flavor.

Makes 4 servings

$1/2$ cup apple juice	Pinch freshly ground black pepper
1 tablespoon + $1^1/2$ teaspoons fresh lemon juice	10 ounces skinless, boneless chicken breast, cut into twenty-four 1" pieces
1 tablespoon honey	3 medium apples, cored and
2 teaspoons vegetable oil	cut into $3/4$" pieces
1 teaspoon curry powder	4 cups cooked white rice, hot
$1/8$ teaspoon salt	

1. Prepare grill for a medium fire, using direct method (see page xiii). Spray grill rack with nonstick cooking spray. If using wooden skewers, soak in water 30 minutes.
2. To prepare marinade, in shallow 13X9" ceramic or glass baking dish, combine apple and lemon juices, honey, oil, curry powder, salt and pepper. Thread 3 pieces chicken onto each of eight 12" metal or wooden skewers; place in dish and spoon marinade over chicken. Cover with plastic wrap; refrigerate 30 minutes, turning skewers after 15 minutes. Remove skewers from marinade.
3. Drain marinade into small saucepan. Bring to a rolling boil; boil for one minute, stirring constantly. Remove from heat.
4. Thread 6 apple pieces onto each of 8 more 12" metal or wooden skewers. Brush apple skewers with marinade and place chicken and apple skewers on prepared rack. Grill, turning occasionally and brushing with remaining marinade, until chicken juices run clear when chicken is pierced with fork and apples are tender, 5–7 minutes.
5. To serve, divide rice evenly among 4 plates; top each serving of rice with 2 chicken and 2 apple kabobs. Spoon any remaining marinade over rice.

Serving (1 cup rice, with 2 ounces chicken and $1/2$ cup apples) provides: $1/2$ Fat, $1^1/4$ Fruits, 2 Proteins, 2 Breads, 15 Optional Calories.

Per serving: 474 Calories, 5 g Total Fat, 1 g Saturated Fat, 48 mg Cholesterol, 117 mg Sodium, 82 g Total Carbohydrate, 3 g Dietary Fiber, 23 g Protein, 44 mg Calcium.

KEY WEST JERK CHICKEN

The term "jerk" simply refers to meat that has been marinated in a spicy sauce and grilled. Here, we've used a flavorful mango-based mixture and slow, low-heat grilling. Pork is also very good when "jerked."

Makes 4 servings

2 medium onions, quartered
1/2 cup chopped scallions
2 Scotch bonnet peppers
  (habanero peppers),* with
  seeds, minced
1 tablespoon ground allspice

1 tablespoon ground thyme
1/2 teaspoon ground nutmeg
1/4 teaspoon salt
1/2 cup cubed mango
Four 5-ounce chicken thighs,
  skinned

1. In food processor, combine onions, scallions, peppers, allspice, thyme, nutmeg and salt; purée until smooth. Add mango; process again until smooth. Thoroughly coat chicken with jerk paste, cover and refrigerate overnight.
2. Prepare grill for a low fire, using direct method (see page xiii).
3. Place chicken on foil or disposable aluminum tray; grill about 45 minutes, turning once. Remove chicken from foil and place directly onto grill; continue grilling an additional 45 minutes, turning once, until jerk paste is crusty. Transfer thighs to each of 4 plates and serve.

Serving (3 ounces chicken) provides: 1/4 Fruit, 3/4 Vegetable, 2 Proteins.

Per serving: 231 Calories, 10 g Total Fat, 3 g Saturated Fat, 81 mg Cholesterol, 217 mg Sodium, 13 g Total Carbohydrate, 2 g Dietary Fiber, 24 g Protein, 66 mg Calcium.

*Scotch bonnet peppers—small green and red peppers with a distinctive bonnet-like shape—are one of the hottest peppers in the world; wear rubber gloves when handling them and wash hands thoroughly afterward. They can be found in many large supermarkets and in Latino and Asian grocery stores. If unavailable, substitute jalapeño peppers.

SUPER-QUICK ORANGE-GLAZED DRUMSTICKS

Nothing could be easier than these drumsticks! It takes only minutes to prepare this delicious glaze; then it's just a matter of firing up the grill for some very good eating.

Makes 4 servings

$^1/_4$ cup orange marmalade
   spreadable fruit
1 tablespoon + 1 teaspoon minced
   fresh thyme leaves
$^1/_2$ teaspoon salt

$^1/_2$ teaspoon extra virgin olive oil
$^1/_4$ teaspoon freshly ground
   black pepper
Four 3-ounce skinless chicken
   drumsticks

1. Prepare grill for a medium fire, using direct method (see page xiii).
2. In small bowl, combine spreadable fruit, thyme, salt, oil and pepper; brush 1 teaspoon glaze on each drumstick.
3. Grill drumsticks, brushing with remaining glaze and turning occasionally, until cooked through and juices run clear when meat is pierced with a fork, 10–12 minutes. Transfer drumsticks to each of 4 plates and serve.

Serving (1 drumstick) provides: 1 Fruit, 1$^1/_2$ Proteins, 5 Optional Calories.

Per serving: 121 Calories, 3 g Total Fat, 1 g Saturated Fat, 40 mg Cholesterol, 314 mg Sodium, 11 g Total Carbohydrate, 0 g Dietary Fiber, 12 g Protein, 14 mg Calcium.

GINGERED CHICKEN KABOBS

You'll love the light sesame-ginger flavors of these quick-to-fix kabobs. Serve them on a bed of brown rice or couscous.

Makes 4 servings

1/4 cup fresh lemon juice
2 tablespoons minced
   fresh cilantro
1 tablespoon minced pared
   fresh ginger root
1 tablespoon reduced-sodium
   soy sauce
2 teaspoons sesame oil

1 teaspoon granulated sugar
10 ounces skinless boneless
   chicken breast, cut into
   1" pieces
1 medium red bell pepper,
   cut into 1" pieces
1/4 medium pineapple,
   cut into chunks

1. Combine lemon juice, cilantro, ginger, soy sauce, oil and sugar; add chicken and marinate at least 2 hours or overnight (see page xvi).
2. Prepare grill for a medium fire, using direct method (see page xiii). If using wooden skewers, soak in water 30 minutes.
3. Drain and discard marinade. Thread chicken, pepper and pineapple evenly onto four 12" metal or wooden skewers.
4. Grill kabobs, turning often, until cooked through, 10–12 minutes. Transfer kabobs to each of 4 plates and serve.

Serving (1 kabob) provides: 1/2 Fat, 1/2 Fruit, 1 Vegetable, 2 Proteins, 5 Optional Calories.

Per serving: 152 Calories, 5 g Total Fat, 1 g Saturated Fat, 48 mg Cholesterol, 196 mg Sodium, 48 g Total Carbohydrate, 1 g Dietary Fiber, 18 g Protein, 17 mg Calcium.

CHICKEN BURGERS

Serve these spicy burgers stuffed into warm Herbed Pita Bread (page 139) or on crusty Italian rolls, with Grilled Peppers (page 161) on the side. A grill basket is convenient but not necessary.

Makes 6 servings

1 pound 3 ounces ground skinless chicken breast

$^1/_4$ cup minced onion

2 tablespoons evaporated skimmed milk

$^1/_2$ teaspoon salt or liquid smoke flavoring

$^1/_2$ teaspoon coarsely ground black pepper

$^1/_2$ teaspoon fennel seeds, crushed

$^1/_2$ teaspoon dried sage leaves, crumbled

1. In medium bowl, combine chicken, onion, evaporated milk, salt or liquid smoke, pepper, fennel seeds and sage. Shape mixture into six $^1/_2$"-thick patties. Cover with plastic wrap and refrigerate until ready to grill.
2. Prepare grill for a medium fire, using direct method (see page xiii).
3. Grill patties directly over coals about 3 minutes; turn and grill 3 minutes longer, until cooked through. Transfer burgers to each of 6 plates and serve immediately.

Serving (1 burger) provides: 2$^1/_2$ Proteins, 4 Optional Calories.

Per serving: 107 Calories, 1 g Total Fat, 0 g Saturated Fat, 52 mg Cholesterol, 247 mg Sodium, 1 g Total Carbohydrate, 0 g Dietary Fiber, 21 g Protein, 31 mg Calcium.

CURRIED CHICKEN–TOFU BURGERS WITH MANGO–PEACH CHUTNEY

Adding a little tofu to the ground chicken makes an uncommonly tender burger. The sweet-spicy chutney is a perfect match for other dishes, too. Consider making a double batch; it will last up to 3 days in the refrigerator.

Makes 4 servings

¹/₂ cup chopped mango chutney
1 large plum tomato, chopped
¹/₂ medium peach, chopped
10 ounces ground skinless chicken breast
4 ounces firm tofu, chopped

¹/₂ cup finely chopped onion
¹/₄ cup finely grated carrot
2 teaspoons curry powder
¹/₄ teaspoon salt
Four 2-ounce hamburger rolls, split
¹/₄ cup plain nonfat yogurt

1. In small bowl, combine chutney, tomato and peach; cover and refrigerate until ready to serve (may be done up to 3 days ahead).
2. Prepare grill for a medium fire, using direct method (see page xiii).
3. In large bowl, combine chicken, tofu, onion, carrot, curry powder and salt. Lightly moisten hands; shape mixture into 4 equal patties.
4. Grill patties directly over coals 5–6 minutes; turn and grill 5–6 minutes longer, until cooked through. Serve each burger on roll with generous ¹/₄ cup of the chutney and 1 tablespoon of the yogurt.

Serving (1 burger on roll, with chutney and yogurt) provides: ¹/₂ Vegetable, 2¹/₂ Proteins, 2 Breads, 75 Optional Calories.

Per serving: 427 Calories, 8 g Total Fat, 2 g Saturated Fat, 48 mg Cholesterol, 895 mg Sodium, 62 g Total Carbohydrate, 2 g Dietary Fiber, 28 g Protein, 187 mg Calcium.

GRILLED TURKEY BURGERS WITH ROASTED ONION TOPPING

This onion topping can also be used to jazz up other simple meat dishes.

Makes 4 servings

2 medium onions
$^1/_2$ cup apple juice
1 tablespoon ketchup
1 tablespoon Dijon-style mustard
1 tablespoon balsamic vinegar

10 ounces ground skinless turkey breast
$^1/_2$ teaspoon salt
$^1/_2$ teaspoon freshly ground black pepper

1. Prepare grill for a medium fire, using direct method (see page xiii); spray grill basket with nonstick cooking spray.
2. Cut onions into $^1/_2$" slices; do not separate into rings. Spray onion slices lightly with nonstick cooking spray and grill in grill basket over hot coals, 3 minutes per side. Remove from heat and dice.
3. In medium saucepan, combine onions, apple juice, ketchup, mustard and vinegar; simmer, covered, 30 minutes. Uncover and simmer 5 minutes more. Set aside.
4. Meanwhile, in medium bowl, combine turkey, salt and pepper; shape mixture into 4 equal patties.
5. Grill patties directly over heat 5–6 minutes; turn and grill 5–6 minutes longer, until cooked through. Serve each burger topped with one-fourth of onion mixture.

Serving (2 ounces turkey, with $^1/_4$ cup onions) provides: $^1/_4$ Fruit, $^1/_2$ Vegetable, 2 Proteins, 4 Optional Calories.

Per serving: 171 Calories, 8 g Total Fat, 2 g Saturated Fat, 39 mg Cholesterol, 417 mg Sodium, 9 g Total Carbohydrate, 1 g Dietary Fiber, 15 g Protein, 33 mg Calcium.

TABBOULEH TURKEY BURGERS

With bulgur boosting their fiber, these juicy, Middle Eastern–spiced burgers are a deliciously healthful alternative to the usual beef variety.

Makes 4 servings

10 ounces ground skinless turkey breast
$^3/_4$ cup chopped seeded tomato
$^1/_2$ cup cooked bulgur
$^1/_4$ cup chopped scallions
$^1/_4$ cup plain nonfat yogurt
2 teaspoons minced fresh mint leaves

$^1/_2$ teaspoon ground cumin
$^1/_4$ teaspoon salt
Four 1-ounce whole-wheat pitas, split and grilled
1 medium tomato, cut into 8 slices

1. Prepare grill for a medium fire, using direct method (see page xiii).
2. In large bowl, combine turkey, tomato, bulgur, scallions, yogurt, mint, cumin and salt. Lightly moisten hands; shape mixture into 4 equal patties.
3. Grill patties directly over coals 5–6 minutes; turn and grill 5–6 minutes longer, until cooked through. Serve each burger in pita with two tomato slices.

Serving (1 burger in pita, with 2 tomato slices) provides: 1 Vegetable, 2 Proteins, 1 Bread, 30 Optional Calories.

Per serving: 201 Calories, 5 g Total Fat, 1 g Saturated Fat, 42 mg Cholesterol, 359 mg Sodium, 25 g Total Carbohydrate, 3 g Dietary Fiber, 15 g Protein, 54 mg Calcium.

GRILL-ROASTED WHOLE TURKEY BREAST WITH SAGE

Try this turkey breast next Thanksgiving—or anytime you have a crowd.

Makes 12 servings

2 garlic cloves, minced
1 tablespoon dried sage leaves, crumbled
1 teaspoon salt

$^1\!/_2$ teaspoon freshly ground black pepper
One 3-pound 8-ounce skinless turkey breast, visible fat removed

1. Prepare grill for a medium fire, using indirect method (see page xiii).
2. In small bowl, combine garlic, sage, salt and pepper. Rub turkey breast all over with mixture.
3. Grill turkey, covered, with all grill vents open, 40 minutes, until cooked through and juices run clear when turkey is pierced in thickest part with fork.
4. Cut turkey into 12 equal pieces; divide evenly among 12 plates and serve.

Serving (3 ounces turkey) provides: 3 Proteins.

Per serving: 116 Calories, 1 g Total Fat, 0 g Saturated Fat, 71 mg Cholesterol, 228 mg Sodium, 0 g Total Carbohydrate, 0 g Dietary Fiber, 26 g Protein, 15 mg Calcium.

GRILLED TURKEY CUTLETS WITH CRANBERRY-ORANGE SALSA

This chunky fruit salsa can be made up to one week ahead and frozen; defrost the sauce overnight in the refrigerator.

Makes 4 servings

1 cup cranberries
$^1/_2$ cup chopped scallions
1 small orange, peeled and
   coarsely chopped
2 teaspoons granulated sugar
2 tablespoons fresh orange juice
1 tablespoon + 1 teaspoon
   olive oil

1 tablespoon minced fresh
   thyme leaves
$^1/_2$ teaspoon salt
$^1/_4$ teaspoon freshly ground
   black pepper
Four 5-ounce turkey cutlets,
   trimmed and pounded
   $^1/_4$" thick

1. In food processor, combine cranberries, scallions, orange and sugar; process one minute until coarsely chopped. Transfer to serving bowl and set aside.
2. Combine juice, oil, thyme, salt and pepper; add turkey and marinate in refrigerator 30 minutes (see page xvi).
3. Prepare grill for a medium fire, using direct method (see page xiii).
4. Drain marinade into small saucepan. Bring to a rolling boil; boil for 1 minute, stirring constantly. Remove from heat.
5. Grill turkey 6 minutes, turning once, basting with marinade.
6. Transfer cutlets to each of 4 plates; spoon one-fourth of the cranberry mixture over each and serve.

Serving (4 ounces turkey, with generous $^1/_4$ cup salsa) provides: 1 Fat, $^1/_2$ Fruit, 4 Proteins, 10 Optional Calories.

Per serving: 237 Calories, 5 g Total Fat, 1 g Saturated Fat, 94 mg Cholesterol, 335 mg Sodium, 11 g Total Carbohydrate, 2 g Dietary Fiber, 35 g Protein, 46 mg Calcium.

GRILLED CORNISH HENS WITH RASPBERRY GLAZE

These little birds are meaty and delicate. You can also grill them in advance and serve cold—just remember to start preparations a day ahead. Foil-Wrapped Greens (page 97) or Charred Sweet Potatoes (page 123) are nice accompaniments.

Makes 4 servings

¹/₄ cup low-sodium chicken broth	¹/₂ teaspoon coarsely ground
2 tablespoons raspberry vinegar	pepper
1 tablespoon seedless raspberry jam	Tiny pinch ground cloves
¹/₂ teaspoon dried rosemary	1 tablespoon vegetable oil
leaves, crumbled	Two 1-pound Cornish hens

1. In small saucepan, combine broth, vinegar, jam, rosemary, pepper and cloves; cook over medium heat, stirring frequently, until jam has dissolved. Reserve half of glaze; cover and refrigerate. Add oil to remaining half.
2. Split hens in half lengthwise. Flatten with heel of hand and place in large dish. Pour warm glaze with oil over hens, brushing them on all sides. Cover and refrigerate overnight.
3. Prepare grill for a medium fire, using direct method (see page xiii), placing grill about 4" above coals.
4. Grill hens directly over coals, skin-side down 10 minutes, moving to edge of grill if they brown too rapidly. Turn skin-side up and grill 15 minutes more. Turn again; grill 5 minutes longer, or until cooked through and juices run clear when hens are pierced in thickest part with fork.
5. Remove and discard skin. Transfer hen halves to each of 4 plates. Warm reserved glaze; spoon over grilled hens and serve.

Serving (¹/₂ hen, with 1 tablespoon glaze) provides: ³/₄ Fat, 3 Proteins, 15 Optional Calories.

Per serving: 208 Calories, 10 g Total Fat, 2 g Saturated Fat, 76 mg Cholesterol, 83 mg Sodium, 4 g Total Carbohydrate, 0 g Dietary Fiber, 25 g Protein, 18 mg Calcium.

CORNISH HENS WITH WILD MUSHROOM STUFFING

Cornish hens are a perfect dish when someone special comes to dinner; they are elegant, flavorful and just the right size. Cèpe, shiitake and cremini mushrooms—found in gourmet grocery stores—add an elegant touch; if unavailable, substitute an equal quantity of white mushrooms.

Makes 4 servings

1 medium onion, diced
$^1/_2$ cup chopped cèpe mushrooms
$^1/_2$ cup chopped shiitake
   mushrooms
$^1/_2$ cup chopped cremini
   mushrooms
1 garlic clove, minced
1 tablespoon minced fresh parsley

1 tablespoon red wine vinegar
1 tablespoon balsamic vinegar
$^1/_2$ teaspoon ground thyme
Two 1-pound Cornish hens
$^1/_2$ teaspoon salt
$^1/_2$ teaspoon freshly ground
   black pepper

1. Prepare grill for a medium fire, using indirect method (see page xiii).
2. Spray medium skillet with nonstick cooking spray and place over medium heat 30 seconds. Add onion and cook, stirring constantly, 3 minutes, until wilted. Add all the mushrooms and the garlic and cook, stirring constantly, 5 minutes more. Stir in parsley, red wine and balsamic vinegars and thyme; cook, stirring constantly, 6 minutes, until mushrooms are soft. Set aside and allow to cool completely.
3. Rinse hens thoroughly inside and out; pat dry with paper towels. Discard giblets and remove visible fat. Rub hens inside and out with salt and pepper; fill each cavity with half the mushroom stuffing. Sew up cavities or close with small metal skewers. Tuck wings under breast and truss.
4. Grill hens, covered, with all grill vents open, 40 minutes, until cooked through and juices run clear when thighs are pierced in thickest part with fork.
5. Remove thread or skewers; cut hens in half with poultry shears. Remove and discard skin. Transfer hen halves to each of 4 plates and serve with mushroom stuffing.

Serving ($^1/_2$ hen, with $^1/_4$ cup stuffing) provides: 1 Vegetable, 3 Proteins.

Per serving: 235 Calories, 9 g Total Fat, 2 g Saturated Fat, 101 mg Cholesterol, 374 mg Sodium, 4 g Total Carbohydrate, 1 g Dietary Fiber, 34 g Protein, 31 mg Calcium.

GRILLED SQUABS

These full-flavored birds taste rich but have less fat than most game birds. The squabs are delicious hot or at room temperature. Serve them with Grilled Polenta (page 130) or Corn and Rice Spoonbread (page 141). By our calculation, one 14-ounce squab yields about 4 ounces cooked meat.

Makes 4 servings

Two 14-ounce squabs
4 fluid ounces (¹/₂ cup) dry red wine
2 tablespoons bitter orange marmalade

2 medium garlic cloves, minced
¹/₂ teaspoon dried rosemary, crumbled
¹/₂ teaspoon coarsely ground black pepper

1. Split squabs in half lengthwise and flatten with heel of hand.
2. In medium nonreactive bowl, combine wine, marmalade, garlic, rosemary and pepper. Reserve 2 tablespoons of marinade. Add squab halves to bowl; turn to coat with marinade. Cover and refrigerate at least 2 hours or up to a day ahead, until ready to grill.
3. Prepare grill for a hot fire, using direct method (see page xiii); place grill rack 4" above coals.
4. When grill is very hot, place squabs directly over fire, skin-side up. Grill, turning frequently and basting with any marinade left in bowl, until cooked through and juices run clear when squabs are pierced in thickest part with fork, about 10 minutes.
5. Transfer squab halves to each of 4 plates. Spoon ¹/₂ tablespoon of reserved marinade over each squab half. Remove and discard skin.

Serving (¹/₂ squab, with ¹/₂ tablespoon sauce) provides: 2 Proteins, 50 Optional Calories.

Per serving:* 162 Calories, 6 g Total Fat, 2 g Saturated Fat, 50 mg Cholesterol, 44 mg Sodium, 8 g Total Carbohydrate, 0 g Dietary Fiber, 13 g Protein, 17 mg Calcium.

*Nutrition information was unavailable for skinless cooked squab; an equivalent amount of skinless cooked duck was substituted for analysis.

GRILLED QUAILS

These crisp little birds are so delicious, they don't need much embellishment! By our calculations, one 4-ounce quail yields about $1^1/2$ ounces cooked meat. Be careful not to overcook them—they make for speedy grilling.

Makes 4 servings

Eight 4-ounce quails
4 fluid ounces ($^1/2$ cup) dry red
    or white wine
1 tablespoon + 1 teaspoon
    olive oil
1 large garlic clove, minced

$^1/2$ teaspoon dried thyme leaves,
    crumbled
$^1/2$ teaspoon dried rosemary leaves,
    crumbled
$^1/2$ teaspoon coarsely ground
    black pepper

1. Cut quails up the back; open and flatten with heel of hand. In large nonreactive dish, combine wine, oil, garlic, thyme, rosemary and pepper. Add quails, turning to coat; marinate 30 minutes at room temperature, or cover and marinate in refrigerator for up to 2 hours.
2. Prepare grill for a hot fire, using direct method (see page xiii); place grill rack 4" above coals.
3. Grill quails skin-side up 3 minutes; turn and grill 4–5 minutes longer, until crisp and brown. Transfer 2 quails to each of 4 plates and serve hot or at room temperature. Remove skin before eating.

Serving (2 quails) provides: 1 Fat, 3 Proteins, 25 Optional Calories.

Per serving: 206 Calories, 9 g Total Fat, 2 g Saturated Fat, 0 mg Cholesterol, 56 mg Sodium, 1 g Total Carbohydrate, 0 g Dietary Fiber, 23 g Protein, 24 mg Calcium.

TANDOORI PHEASANT

A 3-pound pheasant, yielding about 12 ounces cooked meat, is the perfect size for an elegant dinner for two couples. Serve this fragrant dish with a rice pilaf, chutney and a platter of sliced cucumbers and tomatoes.

Makes 4 servings

One 3-pound pheasant, skinned
   and cut into 8 equal pieces
³/₄ cup plain nonfat yogurt
1 tablespoon + 1 teaspoon
   peanut oil
2 garlic cloves, minced
1 teaspoon granulated sugar
¹/₂ teaspoon dried oregano

2 teaspoons mild or hot paprika
1 teaspoon ground cumin
¹/₂ teaspoon ground coriander
¹/₂ teaspoon ground cardamom
¹/₂ teaspoon ground turmeric
¹/₂ teaspoon ground red pepper
¹/₄ teaspoon freshly ground
   black pepper

1. Spray a 13×9" baking dish with nonstick cooking spray. Place pheasant pieces in single layer in prepared dish.
2. In small bowl, combine yogurt, oil, garlic, sugar and oregano; set aside.
3. In small skillet over low heat, combine paprika, cumin, coriander, cardamom, turmeric and red and black peppers; toast, stirring constantly, until fragrant, about 3–4 minutes (do not burn). Stir immediately into yogurt mixture. Pour over pheasant, coating evenly; cover with plastic wrap and refrigerate 8 hours or overnight.
4. Prepare grill for a medium fire, using direct method (see page xiii). Line grill rack with double layer of heavy-duty foil and spray with nonstick cooking spray.
5. Arrange pheasant pieces skinned-side down on foil; grill, turning occasionally, until juices run clear when breasts are pierced with fork, 20–25 minutes. Transfer breasts, wings and legs to serving platter. Continue grilling thighs until juices run clear when thighs are pierced with fork, about 5 minutes more. Transfer to platter; cover with foil and let stand 15 minutes before serving to allow juices to settle. Divide evenly among 4 plates and serve.

Serving (3 ounces pheasant) provides: ¹/₄ Milk, 1 Fat, 3 Proteins, 4 Optional Calories.

Per serving: 231 Calories, 9 g Total Fat, 2 g Saturated Fat, 104 mg Cholesterol, 76 mg Sodium, 6 g Total Carbohydrate, 0 g Dietary Fiber, 30 g Protein, 114 mg Calcium.

CAPON WITH CHOCOLATE-CHIPOTLE SAUCE

Capon is a large, succulent bird that lends itself beautifully to covered grilling. These flavorings would also work well with a small turkey, and any leftovers are delicious cold.

Makes 20 servings

Capon:
One 8-pound capon
1 small orange, quartered
2 large garlic cloves, bruised
2 teaspoons chili powder
1 teaspoon dried oregano
$^1/_2$ teaspoon cumin seeds
$^1/_2$ teaspoon cinnamon

$1^1/_2$ cups low-sodium
    chicken broth
1 tablespoon tomato paste
1–3 teaspoons pureed
    chipotles en adobo*
1 tablespoon + 1 teaspoon
    unsweetened cocoa powder

Chocolate-Chipotle Sauce:
1 teaspoon corn oil
$^1/_2$ cup chopped onion
2 garlic cloves, minced

1 teaspoon fine cornmeal
$^1/_2$ teaspoon cinnamon
$^1/_2$ teaspoon ground anise seeds

1. Prepare covered grill for a hot fire, using indirect method (see page xiii).
2. To prepare capon, rinse capon thoroughly inside and out; pat dry with paper towels. Discard giblets and remove visible fat. Stuff capon cavity with orange and garlic.
3. In small bowl, combine chili powder, oregano, cumin and cinnamon. Sprinkle all but 1 teaspoon of spice mixture into capon cavity. Truss or tie with string and rub outside of bird with remaining mixture. Place in roasting pan, with meat thermometer inserted into thickest part of thigh, not touching bone.
4. Place roasting pan on grill over drip pan; cover. Grill capon, covered, with all grill vents open, 1 hour. Baste with pan juices; cover and continue grilling until thermometer reaches 175° F, about 30 minutes longer.
5. Meanwhile, prepare sauce. Place medium skillet over medium heat 30 seconds; heat oil 30 seconds more. Add onion; cook, stirring frequently, until pale gold, about 7 minutes. Add garlic; cook 2 minutes more.
6. Whisk in broth, tomato paste, chipotle purée, cocoa, cornmeal, cinnamon and anise until smooth. Bring to a boil over medium heat, stirring constantly.

Reduce heat to low and simmer, stirring often, 15 minutes. For smooth sauce, purée in food processor or blender. (This may be prepared a day ahead and refrigerated.)

7. Remove capon from grill; cover capon loosely with foil and let stand 15 minutes before carving. Cut capon into 20 equal pieces. Remove skin before eating. Serve with sauce on the side.

Serving (2 ounces meat, with 1 tablespoon sauce) provides: 2 Proteins, 8 Optional Calories.

Per serving: 118 Calories, 5 g Total Fat, 1 g Saturated Fat, 50 mg Cholesterol, 74 mg Sodium, 1 g Total Carbohydrate, 0 g Dietary Fiber, 17 g Protein, 17 mg Calcium.

*Chipotles en adobo—*smoked dried jalapeño peppers in a spicy tomato sauce—*are available in Latino grocery stores and some supermarkets.*

GRILL-SMOKED DUCK BREAST WITH RED CABBAGE

Thanks to wood chips, your grill can impart a wonderfully smoky flavor to duck. Cooking the cabbage takes a long time, but it requires little work and is well worth the while.

Makes 4 servings

4 cups shredded red cabbage
1 cup thinly sliced red onions
2 small apples, pared, cored and diced
1 cup low-calorie cranberry juice cocktail

$^{1}/_{2}$ cup red wine vinegar
Two 5-ounce skinless boneless duck breasts

1. In large saucepan, combine cabbage, onions, apples, juice cocktail and vinegar; cook, covered, over low heat 3 hours, stirring every half hour or so.
2. Soak $^{1}/_{2}$ cup hickory, oak or cherrywood chips in water 15 minutes; prepare grill for a medium-hot fire, using direct method (see page xiii).
3. Drain wood chips and sprinkle over hot coals. Grill duck breasts, covered, over medium-high heat, 3 minutes per side, until cooked through.
4. Thinly slice duck and divide evenly among 4 plates; serve with one-fourth of the cabbage on the side.

Serving (2 ounces duck, with $^{1}/_{2}$ cup cabbage) provides: $^{3}/_{4}$ Fruit, $2^{1}/_{2}$ Vegetables, 2 Proteins.

Per serving: 192 Calories, 7 g Total Fat, 2 g Saturated Fat, 50 mg Cholesterol, 51 mg Sodium, 19 g Total Carbohydrate, 3 g Dietary Fiber, 15 g Protein, 61 mg Calcium.

3

FISH AND SEAFOOD

Teriyaki-Grilled Tuna with Water Chestnuts • Grilled Grouper

Grilled Swordfish Kabobs with Walnut Sauce • Grilled Swordfish in
Lime-Cilantro Marinade

Grilled Red Snapper with Corn Chutney • Red Snapper Fillets with
Julienned Vegetables

Sweet-and-Sour Halibut • Cod Steaks with Tandoori Spices • Cod in Grape Leaves

Spicy Grilled Bluefish • Mustard-Grilled Salmon Steaks • Salmon Burgers

Grilled Sea Scallops with Parsley-Brandy Pesto • Grilled Sea Scallops
with Basil-Tartar Sauce

Spicy Reddened Shrimp with Papaya-Lime Salsa • Grilled Shrimp with
Ginger-Soy Dipping Sauce

Grilled Marinated Calamari • Calamari on Skewers

Grilled Lobster with Creamy Lemon Sauce • Grilled-Roasted Oysters with
Black Pepper Sauce

TERIYAKI-GRILLED TUNA WITH WATER CHESTNUTS

This dish is fast and easy, especially if you make the marinade ahead of time and store it in the refrigerator until you are ready to use it.

Makes 4 servings

$^1/_4$ cup reduced-sodium soy sauce
2 tablespoons rice wine vinegar
1 fluid ounce (2 tablespoons)
   dry sherry
6 medium garlic cloves, minced
1 tablespoon minced pared
   fresh ginger root

2 teaspoons honey
$^1/_4$ teaspoon freshly ground
   black pepper
$^3/_4$ cup water chestnuts
Two 10-ounce tuna steaks

1. Prepare grill for a medium fire, using direct method (see page xiii). If using wooden skewers, soak in water 30 minutes.
2. In small bowl, combine soy sauce, vinegar, sherry, garlic, ginger, honey and pepper.
3. Thread 4 water chestnuts onto each of four 6" metal or wooden skewers, spacing them $^1/_8$" apart. Brush twice with marinade and grill 6–8 minutes, turning skewers and brushing with marinade occasionally.
4. Meanwhile, brush tuna with marinade and grill over high heat, 5 minutes per side, brushing constantly with remaining marinade.
5. Slice tuna $^1/_8$" thick and divide evenly among 4 plates; top with skewered water chestnuts and serve.

Serving (4 ounces tuna, with 4 water chestnuts) provides: 2 Proteins, $^1/_4$ Bread, 20 Optional Calories.

Per serving: 269 Calories, 7 g Total Fat, 2 g Saturated Fat, 54 mg Cholesterol, 660 mg Sodium, 11 g Total Carbohydrate, 0 g Dietary Fiber, 35 g Protein, 12 mg Calcium.

GRILLED GROUPER

Grouper is a delicious white-fleshed fish. A grill basket, sprayed with nonstick cooking spray, provides extra insurance against sticking. Serve with Grilled Potato Wedges and Green Beans in Foil (pages 127 and 96). Like most fish dishes, this is also good cold.

Makes 4 servings

1 fluid ounce (2 tablespoons)
   dry white wine
1 tablespoon white wine vinegar
1 tablespoon olive oil
2 medium garlic cloves, minced
1 teaspoon tomato paste

$^1/_2$ teaspoon dried thyme leaves
$^1/_4$ teaspoon freshly ground
   black pepper
Four 5-ounce grouper steaks,
   at least 1" thick

1. In small bowl, whisk together wine, vinegar, oil, garlic, tomato paste, thyme and pepper. Place fish in nonreactive dish; coat evenly with mixture, cover and let stand 30 minutes.
2. Prepare grill for a medium fire, using direct method (see page xiii); place grill about 4" above coals. Spray grill basket with nonstick cooking spray.
3. Grill fish 10 minutes for each inch of thickness, turning once. Transfer steaks to each of 4 plates and serve at once.

Serving (4 ounces grouper) provides: $^3/_4$ Fat, 2 Proteins, 6 Optional Calories.

Per serving: 164 Calories, 5 g Total Fat, 1 g Saturated Fat, 52 mg Cholesterol, 87 mg Sodium, 1 g Total Carbohydrate, 0 g Dietary Fiber, 28 g Protein, 45 mg Calcium.

GRILLED SWORDFISH KABOBS WITH WALNUT SAUCE

Makes 4 servings

¹/₄ cup low-sodium chicken broth
2 tablespoons fresh lemon juice
1 tablespoon minced fresh dill
2 teaspoons Dijon-style mustard
¹/₂ teaspoon salt
¹/₂ teaspoon freshly ground
  black pepper
1 pound 2 ounces swordfish,
  cut into 1" cubes

1 medium zucchini, cut into
  1" chunks
¹/₂ cup diced red bell pepper
¹/₂ cup diced yellow bell pepper
12 cherry tomatoes
1 ounce walnuts
1 tablespoon chopped onion
2 teaspoons olive oil

1. Combine broth, juice, dill, mustard, ¹/₄ teaspoon of the salt and ¹/₄ teaspoon of the black pepper; add swordfish and marinate at least one hour or overnight (see page xvi).
2. Drain marinade into small saucepan. Bring to a rolling boil; boil for 1 minute, stirring constantly. Remove from heat.
3. Prepare grill for a medium fire, using direct method (see page xiii). If using wooden skewers, soak in water 30 minutes. Preheat oven to 350° F. Spray baking sheet with nonstick cooking spray.
4. Divide fish, zucchini, red and yellow bell peppers and tomatoes into 12 equal amounts. Thread each of twelve 12" metal or wooden skewers with 1 portion of fish and vegetables, alternating pieces in a colorful pattern and ending each with cherry tomato. Sprinkle with remaining ¹/₄ teaspoon each salt and black pepper. Grill kabobs 8 minutes, turning once.
5. Transfer kabobs to baking sheet and bake 5 minutes, until cooked through.
6. Meanwhile, in food processor, combine marinade with walnuts; pulse several times until coarsely chopped. Add onion and oil and process 30 seconds more.
7. Divide kabobs evenly among 4 plates; pour one-fourth of the sauce over each and serve.

Serving (3 kabobs, with ¹/₄ cup sauce) provides: 1 Fat, 2 Vegetables, 2 Proteins, 1 Optional Calorie.

Per serving: 245 Calories, 12 g Total Fat, 2 g Saturated Fat, 50 mg Cholesterol, 461 mg Sodium, 6 g Total Carbohydrate, 1 g Dietary Fiber, 27 g Protein, 29 mg Calcium.

GRILLED SWORDFISH IN LIME-CILANTRO MARINADE

This marinade works well with most white fish. Try it with sea bass or mahi mahi.

Makes 4 servings

4 five-ounce swordfish steaks, 1" thick
2 fluid ounces (¹/₄ cup) dry vermouth
2 tablespoons fresh lime juice
1 tablespoon minced fresh cilantro

1 tablespoon extra virgin olive oil
1 tablespoon light tamari or reduced-sodium soy sauce
¹/₈ teaspoon mixed herb–seasoned salt

1. Prepare grill for a medium fire using direct method (see page xiii).
2. Combine vermouth, juice, cilantro, oil, tamari or soy sauce and seasoned salt; marinate swordfish 1 hour (see page xvi).
3. Drain marinade into small saucepan. Bring to a rolling boil; boil for 1 minute, stirring constantly. Remove from heat.
4. Grill swordfish 8 minutes, turning once, until fish flakes easily when tested with a fork.
5. Place fish on serving platter; spoon marinade over fish and serve.

Serving (4 ounces swordfish, with one-fourth marinade) provides: ³/₄ Fat, 2 Proteins, 20 Optional Calories.

Per serving: 225 Calories, 9 g Total Fat, 2 g Saturated Fat, 55 mg Cholesterol, 349 mg Sodium, 2 g Total Carbohydrate, 0 g Dietary Fiber, 29 g Protein, 9 mg Calcium.

GRILLED RED SNAPPER WITH CORN CHUTNEY

This tropical dish is perfect for a hot summer night.

Makes 4 servings

1 cup cider vinegar
2 tablespoons granulated sugar
2 cups fresh or thawed frozen
   corn kernels
1 cup thinly sliced red onions
$1/4$ cup + 2 tablespoons raisins
$1/4$ teaspoon cinnamon

$1/4$ teaspoon ground cloves
$1/2$ cup drained canned crushed
   pineapple, with 2 tablespoons
   juice
Four 5-ounce red snapper fillets,
   patted dry

1. In medium nonreactive saucepan, combine vinegar and sugar; bring to a boil, stirring constantly to dissolve sugar. Reduce heat; stir in corn, onions, raisins, cinnamon and cloves. Simmer, uncovered, stirring frequently, 20 minutes, until liquid is reduced slightly. Increase heat to high; stir in pineapple. Cook, stirring frequently, 10 minutes longer, until chutney is thickened and syrupy.
2. Meanwhile, prepare grill for a medium fire, using direct method (see page xiii).
3. Grill red snapper 2–3 minutes on each side, turning once, until fish flakes easily when tested with a fork. Transfer fillets to each of 4 plates and serve with chutney.

Serving (4 ounces red snapper, with $1/2$ cup chutney) provides: 1 Fruit, $1/2$ Vegetable, 2 Proteins, 1 Bread, 25 Optional Calories.

Per serving: 322 Calories, 3 g Total Fat, 1 g Saturated Fat, 52 mg Cholesterol, 110 mg Sodium, 45 g Total Carbohydrate, 4 g Dietary Fiber, 33 g Protein, 77 mg Calcium.

RED SNAPPER FILLETS WITH JULIENNED VEGETABLES

This is the perfect low-fat way to cook fish! Experiment with different fish and vegetable combinations.

Makes 4 servings

Four 5-ounce red snapper fillets
$^1/_2$ teaspoon salt
$^1/_4$ teaspoon freshly ground
  black pepper
1 medium zucchini, trimmed and
  julienned
1 medium yellow squash, trimmed
  and julienned

$^1/_2$ small leek, washed, trimmed
  and julienned
1 medium carrot, julienned
2 fluid ounces ($^1/_4$ cup) dry white
  wine
1 tablespoon + 1 teaspoon fresh
  lemon juice

1. Prepare grill for a medium fire, using direct method (see page xiii).
2. Lightly spray four 18" squares of aluminum foil with nonstick cooking spray. Place one fish fillet in center of each foil square and season each with one-fourth of salt and pepper; distribute one-fourth each of the zucchini, squash, leek and carrot evenly over each fillet. Top each with 1 tablespoon wine and 1 teaspoon juice.
3. Make packets by bringing 2 sides of foil up to meet in center and pressing edges together in two $^1/_2$" folds. Then fold edges of each end together in two $^1/_2$" folds. Allowing room for packets to expand, crimp edges together to seal.
4. Grill packets 10 minutes (packets will puff up). Remove packets from grill and open carefully, avoiding steam. Transfer contents to each of 4 plates and serve.

Serving (1 red snapper fillet, with 1$^1/_2$ cups vegetables) provides:
1$^1/_2$ Vegetables, 2 Proteins, 15 Optional Calories.

Per serving: 189 Calories, 3 g Total Fat, 0 g Saturated Fat, 52 mg Cholesterol, 378 mg Sodium, 7 g Total Carbohydrate, 2 g Dietary Fiber, 30 g Protein, 76 mg Calcium.

SWEET-AND-SOUR HALIBUT

Lightly flavored and firm-textured, halibut takes to this Asian treatment beautifully. If unavailable, substitute snapper, cod or any firm, white-fleshed fish.

Makes 6 servings

$^1/_4$ cup honey
2 tablespoons reduced-sodium
   soy sauce
2 tablespoons fresh lemon juice
1 tablespoon Chinese sesame oil*
2 garlic cloves, minced
1 teaspoon ground ginger

$^1/_2$ teaspoon dry mustard
$^1/_2$ teaspoon crushed red
   pepper flakes
$^1/_2$ teaspoon freshly ground
   black pepper
Six 8-ounce halibut steaks

1. Combine honey, soy sauce, juice, oil, garlic, ginger, mustard, pepper flakes and black pepper; add halibut and marinate 1 hour (see page xvi).
2. Prepare grill for a medium fire, using direct method (see page xiii).
3. Remove fish from marinade with tongs; drain marinade into small saucepan. Bring to a rolling boil; boil for 1 minute, stirring constantly. Remove from heat.
4. Grill halibut 8–10 minutes, turning once and brushing with marinade, until fish flakes easily when tested with a fork. Transfer steaks to each of 6 plates and serve.

Serving (6 ounces halibut) provides: $^1/_2$ Fat, 3 Proteins, 40 Optional Calories.

Per serving: 310 Calories, 7 g Total Fat, 1 g Saturated Fat, 70 mg Cholesterol, 318 mg Sodium, 13 g Total Carbohydrate, 0 g Dietary Fiber, 49 g Protein, 108 mg Calcium.

  Available in most grocery stores, Chinese sesame oil adds an intense sesame flavor integral to this dish. If you substitute regular sesame oil or vegetable oil, the flavor will be very different.

COD STEAKS WITH TANDOORI SPICES

The exotic spices in this colorful dish provide a tangy twist to an otherwise mild fish. Marinate the cod overnight for the fullest flavor.

Makes 4 servings

$^1/_4$ cup yogurt cheese*
$^1/_4$ cup fresh lime juice
1 garlic clove
One 1" piece pared fresh
   ginger root
1 tablespoon curry powder
$^1/_4$ teaspoon cinnamon

$^1/_4$ teaspoon ground cumin
$^1/_4$ teaspoon ground red pepper
$^1/_4$ teaspoon red food coloring
   (optional)
$^1/_8$ teaspoon ground cloves
Four 5-ounce cod steaks
4 lime slices, for garnish

1. In blender or food processor, combine yogurt cheese, juice, garlic, ginger, curry powder, cinnamon, cumin, red pepper, food coloring (if using) and cloves; purée until smooth. Marinate cod steaks at least 1 hour or overnight (see page xvi).
2. Prepare grill for a medium fire, using direct method (see page xiii); spray grill basket with nonstick cooking spray.
3. Remove fish from marinade; place in prepared grill basket and baste with some of the remaining marinade. Grill, basting with remaining marinade, 3 minutes per side, until fish flakes easily when tested with a fork.
4. Carefully remove fish from grill basket; remove and discard skin and bones. Transfer steaks to each of 4 plates; garnish with lime slices and serve.

Serving (4 ounces cod) provides: 2 Proteins, 15 Optional Calories.

Per serving: 138 Calories, 1 g Total Fat, 0 g Saturated Fat, 61 mg Cholesterol, 88 mg Sodium, 4 g Total Carbohydrate, 1 g Dietary Fiber, 27 g Protein, 71 mg Calcium.

*To prepare yogurt cheese, spoon $^1/_2$ cup plain nonfat yogurt into coffee filter or cheesecloth-lined strainer; place over bowl. Refrigerate, covered, at least 5 hours or overnight. Discard liquid in bowl. Makes $^1/_4$ cup yogurt cheese.

COD IN GRAPE LEAVES

Like foil, grape leaves eliminate the problem of fish sticking to the grill; unlike foil, grape leaves are edible. These packets can be prepared in the morning and refrigerated until grilling time. Serve with Grilled Tomatoes (page 89), and use Herbed Pita Bread (page 139) to mop up the savory juices. These cod-filled grape leaves are delicious cold, so you might want to grill a few extra.

Makes 4 servings

16 pickled grape leaves, drained
Four 5-ounce boneless cod steaks
  (about 1" thick)
8 paper-thin lemon slices

$^1/_2$ teaspoon dried oregano
$^1/_2$ teaspoon freshly ground
  black pepper
1 tablespoon + 1 teaspoon olive oil

1. In teakettle or saucepan, bring 2 quarts water to a rolling boil. Place grape leaves in colander in sink; pour boiling water over them. Immediately rinse with cold water and drain.
2. Soak kitchen twine in water.
3. Place about 3 leaves, overlapping each other by half, on work surface. Place a cod steak in center. Top with 2 lemon slices, a pinch each of oregano and pepper, and 1 teaspoon olive oil. Wrap fish in leaves (use additional leaves, if needed, to enclose fish completely) and tie crosswise and lengthwise with twine. Repeat to make 4 packets; cover and refrigerate until ready to grill.
4. Prepare grill for a medium fire, using direct method (see page xiii).
5. Grill directly over coals, turning often to avoid charring leaves, about 10 minutes. Remove twine; transfer packets to each of 4 warm plates and serve.

Serving (1 packet) provides: 1 Fat, $^1/_4$ Vegetable, 2 Proteins.

Per serving: 179 Calories, 5 g Total Fat, 1 g Saturated Fat, 61 mg Cholesterol, 877 mg Sodium, 1 g Total Carbohydrate, 0 g Dietary Fiber, 25 g Protein, 111 mg Calcium.

SPICY GRILLED BLUEFISH

Southwestern seasonings work best with a fish that has a lot of flavor on its own, like bluefish. If unavailable, substitute swordfish or tuna.

Makes 4 servings

2 tablespoons fresh lime juice
$^1/_2$ teaspoon ground coriander
$^1/_2$ teaspoon dried oregano
$^1/_2$ teaspoon freshly ground
    black pepper

Four 8-ounce bluefish fillets
    (about $^3/_4$" thick)

1. Prepare grill for a hot fire, using direct method (see page xiii).
2. In 2-quart shallow nonreactive dish, combine juice, coriander, oregano and pepper; add bluefish, turning to coat. Let stand 5 minutes. Remove fish and discard juice mixture.
3. Grill bluefish 3 minutes on each side, until fish flakes easily when tested with a fork. Transfer fillets to each of 4 plates and serve at once.

Serving (6 ounces bluefish) provides: 3 Proteins.

Per serving: 285 Calories, 10 g Total Fat, 2 g Saturated Fat, 134 mg Cholesterol, 136 mg Sodium, 1 g Total Carbohydrate, 0 g Dietary Fiber, 46 g Protein, 21 mg Calcium.

MUSTARD-GRILLED SALMON STEAKS

Cooked on a grill, salmon is so delicious it will even convert those who ordinarily turn up their noses at fish. The mustardy marinade provides a sharp counterpoint to the richness of the fish. Any leftovers can be made into a spectacular salmon salad using capers, minced celery and a little reduced-calorie mayonnaise.

Makes 4 servings

2 fluid ounces (¹/₄ cup)
   dry white wine
¹/₄ cup white wine vinegar
1 garlic clove, peeled and bruised
3 tablespoons Dijon-style
   mustard
2 tablespoons fresh lemon juice
¹/₂ teaspoon coarsely ground
   black pepper

Four 4-ounce salmon steaks,
   at least 1" thick
2 tablespoons + 2 teaspoons
   reduced-calorie mayonnaise
1–2 tablespoons minced fresh
   tarragon

1. In small nonreactive saucepan, combine wine, vinegar and garlic. Boil over high heat until liquid is reduced by half. Discard garlic; whisk in mustard, juice and pepper. Set 1 tablespoon aside.
2. Place salmon in nonreactive dish; coat all sides with mustard mixture. Cover and let stand 30 minutes.
3. Meanwhile, prepare grill for a medium fire, using direct method (see page xiii). Place grill 4" above coals.
4. In small bowl, whisk together reserved mustard mixture, the mayonnaise and tarragon; set aside.
5. Grill salmon 10 minutes for each 1" of thickness, turning once. Transfer steaks to each of 4 plates and serve with reserved sauce.

Serving (3 ounces salmon, with 1 tablespoon sauce) provides: 1 Fat, 3 Proteins, 6 Optional Calories.

Per serving: 208 Calories, 10 g Total Fat, 2 g Saturated Fat, 66 mg Cholesterol, 378 mg Sodium, 3 g Total Carbohydrate, 0 g Dietary Fiber, 23 g Protein, 27 mg Calcium.

SALMON BURGERS

Packaged coleslaw blend (shredded cabbage and carrots) makes this recipe super-fast. For a quick side dish, toss together the remaining slaw with a little mustard, nonfat mayonnaise and some chopped onion.

Makes 4 servings

5 ounces rinsed drained canned pink salmon

1 cup (3 ounces) coleslaw blend

1/4 cup + 2 tablespoons plain dried bread crumbs

1 egg, lightly beaten

2 tablespoons minced fresh cilantro

1 tablespoon nonfat mayonnaise dressing (10 calories per tablespoon)

2 teaspoons yellow mustard

Freshly ground black pepper, to taste

Four 1-ounce hard rolls, split

1. Preheat grill for a medium fire, using direct method (see page xiii).
2. In medium bowl, combine salmon, coleslaw blend, bread crumbs, egg, cilantro, mayonnaise, mustard and pepper; blend with fork. Divide into four 1/3-cup portions and shape each into a 1"-thick patty.
3. Grill patties directly over coals 4–5 minutes; turn and grill 4–5 minutes longer, until well-browned on both sides but juicy in center. Serve each burger on a roll.

Serving (1 burger on roll) provides: 1/2 Vegetable, 1 1/2 Proteins, 1 1/2 Breads, 3 Optional Calories.

Per serving: 204 Calories, 5 g Fat, 1 g Saturated Fat, 67 mg Cholesterol, 493 mg Sodium, 24 g Total Carbohydrate, 1 g Dietary Fiber, 14 g Protein, 157 mg Calcium.

GRILLED SEA SCALLOPS WITH PARSLEY-BRANDY PESTO

Don't be fooled by the small amount of pesto in this recipe. Its flavor is very intense, so a little bit goes a long way.

Makes 4 servings

3/4 cup minced fresh flat-leaf parsley
1/2 ounce goat cheese
1/2 fluid ounce (1 tablespoon) brandy
1/2 ounce walnuts, finely chopped

1 tablespoon fresh lemon juice
1 tablespoon olive oil
1 garlic clove, minced
1 pound 4 ounces large sea scallops

1. Prepare grill for a hot fire, using direct method (see page xiii); spray grill basket with nonstick cooking spray.
2. In food processor, combine parsley, cheese, brandy, walnuts, juice, oil and garlic; purée until smooth.
3. In medium bowl, toss scallops with pesto until well-coated.
4. Grill scallops in prepared grill basket, 1–2 minutes per side, until opaque. Divide evenly among 4 plates and serve.

Serving (4 ounces scallops) provides: 3/4 Fat, 2 Proteins, 30 Optional Calories.

Per serving: 193 Calories, 7 g Total Fat, 1 g Saturated Fat, 50 mg Cholesterol, 251 mg Sodium, 5 g Total Carbohydrate, 1 g Dietary Fiber, 25 g Protein, 61 mg Calcium.

GRILLED SEA SCALLOPS WITH BASIL-TARTAR SAUCE

Scallops make a perfect light and easy meal. These are done in a flash and can be served cold the next day.

Makes 4 servings

3/4 cup yogurt cheese*
2 tablespoons + 2 teaspoons
   reduced-calorie mayonnaise
2 tablespoons fresh lemon juice
2 teaspoons Dijon-style mustard
1/2 teaspoon salt
1/4 teaspoon freshly ground
   black pepper

1/8 teaspoon paprika
1/8 teaspoon hot red pepper sauce
1/4 cup minced fresh basil
2 tablespoons rinsed, drained capers,
   chopped
1 tablespoon finely chopped shallots
1 pound 4 ounces large sea scallops
4 whole basil leaves, for garnish

1. Prepare grill for a hot fire, using direct method (see page xiii); spray grill basket with nonstick cooking spray.
2. In medium bowl, whisk together yogurt cheese, mayonnaise, juice, mustard, 1/4 teaspoon of the salt, 1/8 teaspoon of the black pepper, the paprika and pepper sauce. Stir in minced basil, capers and shallots. Refrigerate, covered, at least 20 minutes.
3. Season scallops on both sides with the remaining 1/4 teaspoon salt and 1/8 teaspoon pepper. Grill scallops in prepared grill basket, 1–2 minutes per side, until opaque.
4. Divide scallops evenly among 4 plates and spoon 1/4 cup sauce alongside each portion; garnish cach with basil leaf and serve.

Serving (4 ounces scallops, with 1/4 cup sauce) provides: 1/2 Milk, 1 Fat, 2 Proteins.

Per serving: 191 Calories, 4 g Total Fat, 1 g Saturated Fat, 51 mg Cholesterol, 762 mg Sodium, 9 g Total Carbohydrate, 0 g Dietary Fiber, 28 g Protein, 167 mg Calcium.

*To prepare yogurt cheese, spoon 1 1/2 cups plain nonfat yogurt into coffee filter or cheesecloth-lined strainer; place over bowl. Refrigerate, covered, at least 5 hours or overnight. Discard liquid in bowl. Makes 3/4 cup yogurt cheese.

SPICY REDDENED SHRIMP WITH PAPAYA-LIME SALSA

You'll love the spicy flavors of this shrimp—and the beautiful color of the papaya.

Makes 4 servings

1½ teaspoon paprika
½ teaspoon dried thyme leaves
½ teaspoon salt
½ teaspoon freshly ground
   black pepper
⅛–¼ teaspoon ground
   red pepper

1 pound 4 ounces large shrimp,
   peeled and deveined
2 cups cubed papaya
¼ cup chopped scallions
1 lime, peeled and diced

1. Prepare grill for a hot fire, using direct method (see page xiii); spray grill basket with nonstick cooking spray.
2. To prepare seasoning, combine paprika, thyme, salt and black and red peppers; add shrimp and toss to coat (see page xvi).
3. Meanwhile, prepare salsa. In small bowl, combine papaya, scallions and lime; set aside.
4. Grill shrimp in prepared basket about 5 minutes, turning once, until pink and cooked through.
5. Spoon ¼ cup salsa onto each of 4 plates; top with one-fourth of the shrimp and serve.

Serving (4 ounces shrimp, with ¼ cup salsa) provides: ½ Fruit, 2 Proteins.

Per serving: 150 Calories, 1 g Total Fat, 0 g Saturated Fat, 221 mg Cholesterol, 531 mg Sodium, 10 g Total Carbohydrate, 1 g Dietary Fiber, 25 g Protein, 79 mg Calcium.

GRILLED SHRIMP WITH GINGER-SOY DIPPING SAUCE

You will get a delicious taste of the Far East with these easy-to-prepare grilled shrimp. Try this sauce with fish and chicken, too.

Makes 4 servings

1/4 cup chopped scallions
2 tablespoons reduced-sodium
  soy sauce
1 tablespoon minced pared
  fresh ginger root
6 medium garlic cloves, minced

1 tablespoon fresh lemon juice
2 teaspoons firmly packed light or
  dark brown sugar
10 ounces large shrimp, peeled
  and deveined

1. Combine scallions, soy sauce, ginger, garlic, juice and sugar; add shrimp and marinate 2 hours (see page xvi).
2. Preheat grill for a medium fire, using direct method (see page xiii); spray grill basket with nonstick cooking spray.
3. Drain marinade into small saucepan; bring to a rolling boil; boil for 1 minute, stirring constantly. Remove from heat. Let cool and pour into small serving bowl.
4. Grill shrimp in prepared basket 4–6 minutes, turning once, until pink and cooked through. Divide evenly among 4 plates and serve with ginger-soy dipping sauce.

Serving (2 ounces shrimp, with 1 tablespoon sauce) provides: 1 Protein, 8 Optional Calories.

Per serving: 84 Calories, 1 g Total Fat, 0 g Saturated Fat, 86 mg Cholesterol, 387 mg Sodium, 6 g Total Carbohydrate, 0 g Dietary Fiber, 12 g Protein, 46 mg Calcium.

GRILLED MARINATED CALAMARI

This unusual way to serve calamari (squid) is quick, easy and tasty. Marinate the squid briefly before cooking, or grill them plain and toss with the marinade as a dressing before serving.

Makes 4 servings

2 tablespoons fresh lemon juice
2 tablespoons red wine vinegar
2 teaspoons Dijon-style mustard
$^1/_2$ teaspoon dried thyme leaves
$^1/_2$ teaspoon salt
$^1/_4$ teaspoon crushed red
 pepper flakes

1 tablespoon + 1 teaspoon olive oil
1 pound 4 ounces cleaned small
 squid
4 lemon wedges, for garnish

1. Prepare grill for a hot fire, using direct method (see page xiii). Spray a grill basket with nonstick cooking spray.
2. In medium bowl, combine juice, vinegar, mustard, thyme, salt and pepper flakes; whisk in oil a little at a time. Add squid and toss well to coat.
3. With slotted spoon, transfer squid to prepared grill basket and grill over high heat, turning constantly and brushing with remaining marinade, 7–9 minutes, until golden and slightly charred.
4. Slice squid into $^1/_2$" pieces. Divide evenly among 4 warm plates, garnish with lemon wedges and serve.

Serving (4 ounces squid) provides: 1 Fat, 2 Proteins.

Per serving: 176 Calories, 6 g Total Fat, 1 g Saturated Fat, 331 mg Cholesterol, 398 mg Sodium, 5 g Total Carbohydrate, 0 g Dietary Fiber, 22 g Protein, 52 mg Calcium.

CALAMARI ON SKEWERS

Calamari (squid) can also be grilled in a wire grill basket; just be sure to spray the squid well with nonstick cooking spray. Be careful not to overcook squid; they will become impossibly rubbery.

Makes 4 servings

4 fluid ounces (¹/₂ cup)
   medium dry sherry
¹/₄ cup reduced-sodium soy sauce
¹/₄ cup fresh lemon juice
1 tablespoon peanut oil
4 medium garlic cloves, crushed

1 teaspoon light sesame oil
1 teaspoon hot red pepper sauce,
   or to taste
1 pounds 4 ounces cleaned
   small squid
Lemon wedges, to garnish

1. In medium bowl, combine sherry, soy sauce, juice, peanut oil, garlic, sesame oil and pepper sauce, whisking to blend. Set aside ¹/₂ cup of marinade for dipping sauce. Add squid to remaining marinade; toss to coat. Cover and let stand 30 minutes at room temperature.
2. Meanwhile, prepare grill for a medium fire, using direct method (see page xiii). If using wooden skewers, soak in water 30 minutes.
3. Thread squid onto twelve 12" metal or wooden skewers. Grill directly over hot coals, just until squid becomes opaque, about 2–3 minutes each side. Place 3 kabobs on each of 4 plates and serve immediately with lemon wedges and reserved dipping sauce.

Serving (4 ounces squid, with 2 tablespoons sauce) provides: 1 Fat, 2 Proteins, 45 Optional Calories.

Per serving: 232 Calories, 7 g Total Fat, 1 g Saturated Fat, 330 mg Cholesterol, 701 mg Sodium, 11 g Total Carbohydrate, 0 g Dietary Fiber, 23 g Protein, 56 mg Calcium.

GRILLED LOBSTER WITH CREAMY LEMON SAUCE

The key to great lobster is to get the freshest you can find; buy it just before you're ready to cook and have the fishmonger split and clean it for you.

Makes 4 servings

³/₄ cup yogurt cheese*
2 tablespoons minced fresh dill
2 tablespoons fresh lemon juice
³/₈ teaspoon freshly ground
  black pepper

Two 1¹/₂-pound lobsters, split
  and cleaned
¹/₄ teaspoon salt
4 lemon slices, for garnish

1. Prepare grill for a medium fire, using direct method (see page xiii).
2. In medium bowl, combine yogurt cheese, dill, juice and ¹/₄ teaspoon of the pepper; stir to blend. Set aside.
3. Season lobsters with salt and remaining ¹/₈ teaspoon pepper. Break lobster claws off and crack with back of a heavy knife. Place lobsters on grill, split-side down; place claws on slightly cooler part of grill and cover loosely with foil. Grill 8–10 minutes, until meat is firm.
4. Remove lobsters from grill and separate halves; crack claws through completely. Place half a lobster and one claw on each of 4 plates. Garnish with lemon slices and serve with one-fourth of the sauce on the side.

Serving (3 ounces lobster, with 3 tablespoons sauce) provides: ¹/₂ Milk, 1¹/₂ Proteins.

Per serving: 117 Calories, 1 g Total Fat, 0 g Saturated Fat, 61 mg Cholesterol, 491 mg Sodium, 5 g Total Carbohydrate, 0 g Dietary Fiber, 21 g Protein, 170 mg Calcium.

To prepare yogurt cheese, spoon 1¹/₂ cups plain nonfat yogurt into coffee filter or cheesecloth-lined strainer; place over bowl. Refrigerate, covered, at least 5 hours or overnight. Discard liquid in bowl. Makes ³/₄ cup yogurt cheese.

GRILL-ROASTED OYSTERS WITH BLACK PEPPER SAUCE

This is heavenly fare for an early fall picnic: simple, almost primitive and utterly delicious. True oyster lovers need no side dishes, but cold light beer or dry white wine would be lovely. You might precede the feast with Roast Corn Chowder (page 12) to placate extra-hungry guests.

Makes 4 servings

4 fluid ounces ($^1/_2$ cup)
  dry white vermouth
1 teaspoon or more freshly
  cracked black pepper
$^1/_2$ cup white wine vinegar
1 tablespoon minced shallots
  or scallions

4 dozen medium oysters, scrubbed
  and rinsed well
Hot red pepper sauce, to taste
Lemon wedges, for garnish

1. Prepare grill for a medium fire, using direct method (see page xiii). Place grill 4–5" above coals.
2. In small nonreactive saucepan, heat vermouth to a simmer. Add pepper; remove from heat and stir in vinegar and shallots. Let stand until cool.
3. Grill oysters, flat-side up, 3–5 minutes, until they open. Discard any that do not open after 5 minutes. Using an oven mitt to hold oyster, pry off top shell with oyster knife or rounded end of "church key"–type bottle opener. Divide oysters evenly among 4 plates and serve with black pepper sauce, red pepper sauce and lemon wedges.

Serving (12 oysters, with $^1/_4$ cup sauce) provides: 2 Proteins, 25 Optional Calories.

Per serving: 116 Calories, 3 g Total Fat, 1 g Saturated Fat, 62 mg Cholesterol, 129 mg Sodium, 6 g Total Carbohydrate, 0 g Dietary Fiber, 8 g Protein, 57 mg Calcium.

MEATS

Grilled Marinated London Broil • Herbed Beef Tenderloin

Grilled Flank Steak Roulade • Grilled Deviled Flank Steak • Asian Beef on a Stick

Grilled Marinated Butterflied Leg of Lamb • Grilled Lamb Chops with
Tomato-Mint Chutney

Jalapeño-Nut–Crusted Lamb Chops • Grilled Veal Chops with Balsamic Glaze

Grilled Loin of Veal with Lemon-Caper Sauce • Tuscan Grilled Pork

Pork Chops with Indian Spices • Pork Cutlets with Apples and Onions

Marsala-Barbecued Spareribs • Middle Eastern Meatball Kabobs
with Yogurt Sauce

Italian Burgers • Barbecued Beef and Lentil Burgers • Kansas City
Barbecued Beef on a Bun

Lone Star Brisket Sandwiches • Gaucho Brisket

GRILLED MARINATED LONDON BROIL

The piquant flavor of this marinade comes from the blending of three different types of vinegar.

Makes 4 servings

One 15-ounce lean London
  broil, 1" thick
$^1/_2$ cup finely chopped onion
$^1/_4$ cup sherry vinegar
$^1/_4$ cup red wine vinegar
2 fluid ounces ($^1/_4$ cup) dry
  red wine
2 tablespoons reduced-sodium
  soy sauce
1 tablespoon balsamic vinegar
6 medium garlic cloves,
  coarsely chopped

2 teaspoons olive oil
Sugar substitute to equal
  1 tablespoon + 1 teaspoon sugar
1 teaspoon grated pared fresh
  ginger root or 1 teaspoon
  ground ginger
Freshly ground black pepper,
  to taste
8 scallions, trimmed

1. Let steak stand, covered, at room temperature 30 minutes.
2. Combine onion, sherry and red wine vinegars, wine, soy sauce, balsamic vinegar, garlic, oil, sugar substitute, ginger and black pepper and marinate steak 4 hours, turning steak after 2 hours (see page xvi). Remove steak with tongs, reserving marinade.
3. In small saucepan over high heat, bring marinade to a rolling boil; boil for 1 minute, stirring constantly. Remove from heat and set aside.
4. Prepare grill for a hot fire, using direct method (see page xiii); spray grill with nonstick cooking spray.
5. Grill steak, basting with marinade, 5–7 minutes on each side (rare), 7–9 minutes (medium-rare), 9–10 minutes (medium), 10–12 minutes (well-done). Remove from heat; let stand 5 minutes before slicing. Divide evenly among 4 plates; garnish each with 2 scallions and serve.

Serving (3 ounces beef, with 2 scallions) provides: $^1/_2$ Fat, $^1/_2$ Vegetable, 3 Proteins, 15 Optional Calories.

Per serving: 213 Calories, 9 g Total Fat, 2 g Saturated Fat, 66 mg Cholesterol, 256 mg Sodium, 5 g Total Carbohydrate, 0 g Dietary Fiber, 25 g Protein, 14 mg Calcium.

HERBED BEEF TENDERLOIN

Few things are more elegant than beef tenderloin. Thinly sliced, this wonderful cut is perfect for a special summer evening. Take care not to overcook the tenderloin.

Makes 4 servings

¹/₄ cup minced fresh parsley
1 tablespoon minced fresh
   rosemary leaves
1 tablespoon Dijon-style mustard
4 medium garlic cloves, minced
1 teaspoon minced fresh
   thyme leaves

1 teaspoon olive oil
¹/₂ teaspoon freshly ground
   black pepper
One 15-ounce trimmed
   beef tenderloin

1. In small bowl, combine parsley, rosemary, mustard, garlic, thyme, oil and pepper. Spread on beef tenderloin; wrap beef in plastic wrap and set aside at room temperature 30 minutes.
2. Meanwhile, preheat grill for a medium fire, using direct method (see page xiii).
3. Grill beef, turning frequently, 20 minutes (rare), 22 minutes (medium) or 24 minutes (well-done). Remove from heat; let stand 10 minutes before slicing. Divide evenly among 4 plates and serve.

Serving (3 ounces beef) provides: ¹/₄ Fat, 3 Proteins.

Per serving: 198 Calories, 10 g Total Fat, 3 g Saturated Fat, 71 mg Cholesterol, 146 mg Sodium, 1 g Total Carbohydrate, 0 g Dietary Fiber, 24 g Protein, 19 mg Calcium.

GRILLED FLANK STEAK ROULADE

With flecks of parsley, pine nuts and raisins woven through the center of the meat, this makes a pretty presentation.

Makes 4 servings

One 15-ounce trimmed
   flank steak
$1/4$ teaspoon salt
$1/4$ teaspoon freshly ground
   black pepper
1 garlic clove, minced

1 tablespoon raisins,
   coarsely chopped
1 ounce pine nuts (pignolia),
   coarsely chopped
2 teaspoons coarsely chopped
   fresh flat-leaf parsley

1. Prepare grill for a medium fire, using direct method (see page xiii).
2. Season steak with salt and pepper; evenly distribute garlic, raisins, pine nuts and parsley over 1 side of steak. Starting at smaller end, tightly roll up steak jelly-roll fashion. Secure lengthwise with metal skewer; close ends with toothpicks to keep filling enclosed.
3. Grill steak 25–30 minutes, turning to brown well on all sides. Remove from heat; let stand 5 minutes before slicing. Remove skewer and toothpicks; carefully carve meat so that each slice stays intact. Divide evenly among 4 plates and serve.

Serving (one-fourth of roulade) provides: $1/2$ Fat, 3 Proteins, 10 Optional Calories.

Per serving: 206 Calories, 11 g Total Fat, 4 g Saturated Fat, 52 mg Cholesterol, 201 mg Sodium, 3 g Total Carbohydrate, 1 g Dietary Fiber, 23 g Protein, 12 mg Calcium.

GRILLED DEVILED FLANK STEAK

This steak with vegetables is full of rich, spicy flavor. Any leftovers are delicious layered in a hearty sandwich.

Makes 4 servings

1 tablespoon + 1 teaspoon
   reduced-calorie tub margarine
1 tablespoon plain dried
   bread crumbs
1 tablespoon minced scallion
1 tablespoon grainy mustard

1 teaspoon Worcestershire sauce
2 cups sliced green bell peppers
2 medium tomatoes, cut into
   $^1/_4$" slices
One 15-ounce trimmed
   flank steak

1. Prepare grill for a medium fire, using direct method (see page xiii); spray grill basket with nonstick cooking spray.
2. In small bowl, combine margarine, bread crumbs, scallion, mustard and Worcestershire sauce; set aside.
3. Arrange peppers and tomatoes in prepared grill basket. Place steak on grill; grill steak and vegetables 5 minutes. Turn steak and vegetables; spread top of steak with margarine mixture. Grill 5 minutes longer, or until steak and vegetables are done to taste. Remove from heat; let steak stand 5 minutes before carving across the grain into thin diagonal slices. Divide evenly among 4 plates and serve with one-fourth of the vegetables.

Serving (3 ounces beef, with one-fourth vegetables) provides: $^1/_2$ Fat, 2 Vegetables, 3 Proteins, 5 Optional Calories.

Per serving: 235 Calories, 11 g Total Fat, 4 g Saturated Fat, 57 mg Cholesterol, 178 mg Sodium, 9 g Total Carbohydrate, 2 g Dietary Fiber, 25 g Protein, 19 mg Calcium.

ASIAN BEEF ON A STICK

Serve these beef kabobs on a bed of grated carrot and shredded lettuce for a different dinner entrée.

Makes 4 servings

$^1/_4$ cup chopped scallions
2 tablespoons reduced-sodium
soy sauce
1 tablespoon minced pared
fresh ginger root
1 tablespoon rice wine vinegar
2 teaspoons sesame oil

1 teaspoon balsamic vinegar
$^1/_2$ teaspoon freshly ground
black pepper
1 garlic clove, minced
10 ounces lean beef loin,
cut into 16 strips
$^1/_4$ cup Chinese mustard

1. Prepare grill for a hot fire, using direct method (see page xiii). If using wooden skewers, soak in water 30 minutes.
2. Combine scallions, soy sauce, ginger, rice wine vinegar, oil, balsamic vinegar, pepper and garlic; add beef and marinate 15 minutes (see page xvi).
3. Remove beef from marinade with tongs; discard any remaining marinade. On each of sixteen 6" metal or wooden skewers, thread 1 beef strip by piercing beef in several places. Grill kabobs 5 minutes, then turn and grill 5 minutes more. Place 4 kabobs on each of 4 plates and serve with Chinese mustard on the side.

Serving (4 kabobs, with 1 tablespoon mustard) provides: $^1/_2$ Fat, 2 Proteins.

Per serving: 141 Calories, 6 g Total Fat, 2 g Saturated Fat, 50 mg Cholesterol, 338 mg Sodium, 1 g Total Carbohydrate, 0 g Dietary Fiber, 18 g Protein, 11 mg Calcium.

GRILLED MARINATED BUTTERFLIED LEG OF LAMB

This recipe can be halved by making half a batch of marinade, cutting the butterflied leg of lamb in two and freezing half for another time.

Makes 8 servings

One 1-pound 8-ounce trimmed
   boneless leg of lamb
1/2 cup red wine vinegar
1/4 cup diced red onion
1/4 cup minced fresh mint
1/4 cup minced fresh parsley

2 fluid ounces (1/4 cup)
   dry red wine
1 tablespoon + 1 teaspoon
   Dijon-style mustard
1/4 teaspoon freshly ground
   black pepper

1. As though you were cutting a loaf of French bread, cut the leg of lamb almost in half lengthwise to create a flattened piece of lamb uniformly 1/2" thick when "opened."
2. Combine vinegar, onion, mint, parsley, wine, mustard and pepper; add lamb and marinate at least 2 hours or overnight (see page xvi).
3. Prepare grill for a medium-hot fire, using direct method (see page xiii).
4. Drain marinade into small saucepan. Bring to a rolling boil; boil for one minute, stirring constantly. Remove from heat.
5. Grill lamb, basting with marinade and turning once, 18 minutes (medium) or 20 minutes (well-done). Spoon remaining marinade over meat; cover with foil and let stand 10 minutes before slicing. Divide evenly among 4 plates and serve.

Serving (2 ounces lamb) provides: 2 Proteins, 6 Optional Calories.

Per serving: 121 Calories, 4 g Total Fat, 2 g Saturated Fat, 50 mg Cholesterol, 100 mg Sodium, 1 g Total Carbohydrate, 0 g Dietary Fiber, 16 g Protein, 10 mg Calcium.

GRILLED LAMB CHOPS WITH TOMATO-MINT CHUTNEY

This satisfying main dish combines the coolness of mint with the heat of red pepper. Make the chutney up to two days ahead and store it, covered, in the refrigerator.

Makes 4 servings

1 tablespoon + 1 teaspoon
   olive oil
$^1/_2$ cup chopped onion
2 garlic cloves, minced
4 small plum tomatoes,
   chopped
$^1/_2$ cup diced yellow bell pepper
$^1/_4$ teaspoon salt
$^1/_4$ teaspoon freshly ground
   black pepper

2 tablespoons minced
   fresh mint leaves
2 tablespoons fresh lime juice
$^1/_8$–$^1/_4$ teaspoon crushed
   red pepper flakes
Four 5-ounce trimmed loin
   lamb chops, $^3/_4$" thick

1. Place medium nonstick skillet over medium-high heat 30 seconds; heat oil 30 seconds more. Add onion and garlic; cook, stirring frequently, until soft, about 2 minutes. Add tomatoes, bell pepper, salt and black pepper; cook, stirring, until pepper is tender-crisp, about 3 minutes. Remove from heat.
2. Transfer vegetable mixture to small bowl. Stir in mint, juice and pepper flakes, to taste; set chutney aside.
3. Prepare grill for a medium fire, using direct method (see page xiii).
4. Grill chops, turning once, 4–5 minutes (rare), 6–7 minutes (medium) or 8–9 minutes (well-done).
5. Transfer chops to each of 4 warm plates and spoon $^1/_2$ cup chutney over each chop before serving.

Serving (3 ounces lamb, with $^1/_2$ cup chutney) provides: 1 Fat, 1 Vegetable, 3 Proteins.

Per serving: 245 Calories, 13 g Total Fat, 4 g Saturated Fat, 81 mg Cholesterol, 211 mg Sodium, 5 g Total Carbohydrate, 1 g Dietary Fiber, 26 g Protein, 29 mg Calcium.

JALAPEÑO-NUT—CRUSTED LAMB CHOPS

Jelly is the secret to making the walnuts stick; substitute mint jelly for the spicy jalapeño, if you prefer.

Makes 4 servings

Four 5-ounce trimmed loin
  lamb chops, 1 1/2" thick
1 tablespoon + 1 teaspoon jalapeño
  or mint jelly
1 garlic clove, finely minced

1/8 teaspoon salt
1/8 teaspoon freshly ground
  black pepper
1/2 ounce walnuts, finely chopped

1. Prepare grill for a medium fire, using direct method (see page xiii).
2. Grill chops about 10 minutes (medium), turning once.
3. Meanwhile, in small bowl, combine jelly, garlic, salt and pepper. Transfer chops to each of 4 warm plates; with pastry brush, coat all sides of chops with jelly mixture. Sprinkle walnuts evenly over chops to form a nut crust before serving.

Serving (1 lamb chop, with crust) provides: 1/4 Fat, 3 Proteins, 25 Optional Calories.

Per serving: 224 Calories, 10 g Total Fat, 3 g Saturated Fat, 81 mg Cholesterol, 143 mg Sodium, 5 g Total Carbohydrate, 0 g Dietary Fiber, 26 g Protein, 21 mg Calcium.

GRILLED VEAL CHOPS WITH BALSAMIC GLAZE

Veal chops make an elegant entrée for any occasion.

Makes 4 servings

1/4 cup balsamic vinegar
3 tablespoons fresh lemon juice
1 tablespoon Worcestershire sauce
2 teaspoons Dijon-style mustard
2 teaspoons honey

Four 3-ounce loin veal chops
1/2 teaspoon salt
1/4 teaspoon freshly ground
    black pepper

1. Prepare grill for a hot fire, using direct method (see page xiii).
2. To prepare glaze, in small bowl, combine vinegar, juice, Worcestershire sauce, honey and mustard.
3. Season chops with salt and pepper and brush with glaze. Grill over high heat, brushing with remaining glaze, 3 minutes per side. Transfer chops to each of 4 warm plates and serve.

Serving (2 ounces veal) provides: 2 Proteins, 10 Optional Calories.

Per serving: 121 Calories, 4 g Total Fat, 1 g Saturated Fat, 60 mg Cholesterol, 433 mg Sodium, 5 g Total Carbohydrate, 0 g Dietary Fiber, 15 g Protein, 16 mg Calcium.

GRILLED LOIN OF VEAL WITH LEMON-CAPER SAUCE

Lemon and capers are the perfect complement to veal. This dish can also be served cold when the weather is hot.

Makes 4 servings

One 10-ounce boneless loin of veal
1 teaspoon salt
1 teaspoon freshly ground
    black pepper
1 teaspoon olive oil
1 tablespoon minced shallots

$^1/_4$ cup low-sodium chicken broth
2 tablespoons rinsed drained capers
$^1/_2$ teaspoon minced lemon zest*
2 tablespoons fresh lemon juice
2 teaspoons arrowroot** mixed
    with 2 teaspoons water

1. Prepare grill for a medium fire, using indirect method (see page xiii).
2. Season veal with salt and pepper; grill, covered, 15 minutes.
3. Meanwhile, place small saucepan over medium heat 30 seconds; heat oil 30 seconds more. Add shallots and cook, stirring constantly, 3 minutes. Add broth, capers, zest and juice. Bring to a boil, reduce heat and simmer 2 minutes. Whisk in arrowroot mixture; simmer, stirring constantly, 30 seconds, until thickened. Set aside and keep warm.
4. Thinly slice veal. Divide evenly among 4 plates and spoon sauce evenly over veal before serving.

Serving (2 ounces veal, with 3 tablespoons sauce) provides: $^1/_4$ Fat, 2 Proteins, 6 Optional Calories.

Per serving: 121 Calories, 5 g Total Fat, 2 g Saturated Fat, 60 mg Cholesterol, 722 mg Sodium, 3 g Total Carbohydrate, 0 g Dietary Fiber, 15 g Protein, 21 mg Calcium.

The zest of the lemon is the peel without any of the pith (white membrane). To remove zest from lemon, use a zester or vegetable peeler.

**Arrowroot is a fine powdered starch used for thickening. It is mixed with cold liquid to form a paste before being stirred into hot mixtures. If unavailable, substitute an equal amount of cornstarch or potato starch or substitute 1 tablespoon + 1 teaspoon flour. If using flour, add 10 Optional Calories per serving.*

TUSCAN GRILLED PORK

The flavors of northern Italy—rosemary, sage and garlic—are delicious with chicken as well as pork. If you substitute skinless boneless chicken breast for the pork in this recipe, marinate the chicken for only 30 minutes. Grilled tomatoes and a tossed green salad make very easy accompaniments.

Makes 4 servings

4 fluid ounces ($^1/_2$ cup) dry white wine

2 teaspoons vegetable oil

1 teaspoon dried rosemary leaves, crumbled

1 large garlic clove, minced

$^1/_2$ teaspoon dried sage leaves, crumbled

$^1/_8$ teaspoon salt

$^1/_8$ teaspoon freshly ground black pepper

10 ounces trimmed lean pork tenderloin, cut into twenty-four $^3/_4$" pieces

4 cups cooked white rice, hot

1. Prepare grill for a medium fire, using direct method (see page xiii). If using wooden skewers, soak in water 30 minutes.
2. To prepare marinade, in 13×9" nonreactive baking dish, combine wine, oil, rosemary, garlic, sage, salt and pepper. Thread 3 pieces of pork onto each of eight 12" metal or wooden skewers; place in dish and spoon marinade over pork. Cover with plastic wrap; refrigerate 1 hour, turning after 30 minutes. Remove pork from marinade.
3. Drain marinade into small saucepan. Bring to a rolling boil; boil for one minute, stirring constantly. Remove from heat.
4. Grill kabobs, turning occasionally and brushing with marinade, until juices run clear when pierced with fork, 5–7 minutes. Discard any remaining marinade.
5. Divide rice evenly among 4 plates; top each portion of rice with 2 kabobs and serve.

Serving (2 ounces pork, with 1 cup rice) provides: $^1/_2$ Fat, 2 Proteins, 2 Breads, 25 Optional Calories.

Per serving: 413 Calories, 6 g Total Fat, 2 g Saturated Fat, 53 mg Cholesterol, 112 mg Sodium, 58 g Total Carbohydrate, 1 g Dietary Fiber, 23 g Protein, 35 mg Calcium.

PORK CHOPS WITH INDIAN SPICES

This delicately flavored marinade imparts the fragrant flavors of India to the pork and tenderizes the meat at the same time. The marinade is also great on skinless chicken parts.

Makes 4 servings

2 tablespoons plain nonfat yogurt
2 teaspoons honey
2 medium garlic cloves, minced
1 teaspoon white wine vinegar
$1/2$ teaspoon ground cumin
$1/2$ teaspoon grated pared fresh
   ginger root

$1/4$ teaspoon ground turmeric
$1/4$ teaspoon salt
$1/8$ teaspoon ground cloves
$1/8$ teaspoon cinnamon
$1/8$ teaspoon ground red pepper
Four 5-ounce pork chops

1. Combine yogurt, honey, garlic, vinegar, cumin, ginger, turmeric, salt, cloves, cinnamon and red pepper; add pork and marinate at least 2 hours (see page xvi).
2. Prepare grill for a medium fire, using direct method (see page xiii). Spray grill rack with nonstick cooking spray.
3. Grill pork chops about 8 minutes, turning once, until cooked through and juices run clear when meat is pierced with fork. Transfer chops to each of 4 warm plates and serve.

Serving (3 ounces pork) provides: 3 Proteins, 15 Optional Calories.

Per serving: 190 Calories, 7 g Total Fat, 3 g Saturated Fat, 70 mg Cholesterol, 192 mg Sodium, 4 g Total Carbohydrate, 0 g Dietary Fiber, 26 g Protein, 47 mg Calcium.

PORK CUTLETS WITH APPLES AND ONIONS

Apples and onions are the perfect match for grilled pork; you can even cook them ahead and heat just prior to grilling the meat.

Makes 4 servings

Four 4-ounce lean boneless
  pork cutlets
$^1/_2$ teaspoon salt
$^1/_2$ teaspoon freshly ground
  black pepper
$^1/_2$ teaspoon onion powder
3 tablespoons Dijon-style
  mustard

2 teaspoons reduced-calorie
  tub margarine
1 medium onion, sliced into
  $^1/_4$" rings
$^1/_2$ cup apple juice
1 small Granny Smith apple,
  pared, cored and cut into
  $^1/_4$" rings

1. Prepare grill for a medium-hot fire, using direct method (see page xiii). Spray grill rack with nonstick cooking spray.
2. Season both sides of pork cutlets evenly with salt, pepper and onion powder; brush both sides evenly with mustard and set aside.
3. Place medium nonstick skillet over medium heat 30 seconds; melt margarine 30 seconds more. Add onion and cook, stirring frequently, 10 minutes. Add apple juice and simmer 3 minutes. Add apple rings and cook 5 minutes more. Remove from heat and keep warm.
4. Grill cutlets 6 minutes per side, until cooked through and juices run clear when meat is pierced with fork. Transfer cutlets to each of 4 warm plates, spoon $^1/_4$ apple mixture over each cutlet and serve.

Serving (3 ounces pork, with $^1/_4$ cup apple mixture) provides: $^1/_4$ Fat, $^1/_2$ Fruit, $^1/_4$ Vegetable, 3 Proteins.

Per serving: 242 Calories, 11 g Total Fat, 4 g Saturated Fat, 80 mg Cholesterol, 493 mg Sodium, 10 g Total Carbohydrate, 1 g Dietary Fiber, 25 g Protein, 27 mg Calcium.

MARSALA-BARBECUED SPARERIBS

This recipe combines a dry rub with a slightly sweet "mop" sauce, brushed on at the end of the cooking. If you like a very smoky flavor, add a second handful of hickory or mesquite chips after an hour of cooking. Do not add the soaked chips at the same time you add the briquets or you may put out the fire!

Makes 12 servings

1 tablespoon + 1 teaspoon firmly packed dark brown sugar

2 teaspoons freshly ground black pepper

2 teaspoons dry mustard

2 teaspoons paprika

1 teaspoon garlic powder

1 teaspoon cinnamon

1 teaspoon ground red pepper, or to taste

$^1/_2$ teaspoon ground cumin

$^1/_4$ teaspoon ground cloves

One 12-rib well-trimmed rack pork spareribs (about 3 pounds)

2 cups Marsala Barbecue Sauce (page 151)

1. In small bowl, combine sugar, black pepper, mustard, paprika, garlic powder, cinnamon, red pepper, cumin and cloves. Place ribs on large sheet of plastic wrap and coat on all sides with spice mixture. Wrap and refrigerate 8–12 hours.
2. If using hickory or other chips, soak in water 30 minutes. Prepare covered grill for a medium fire, using indirect method (see page xiii). When coals are ready, place ribs on grill over drip pan. Close cover, with bottom vents open and top vents half open.
3. Grill spareribs 30 minutes, then add drained wood chips, if using. Grill 60 minutes longer (adding additional briquets if needed) until meat falls easily off bone.
4. Brush ribs with about half the Marsala Barbecue Sauce; grill, uncovered, 5–10 minutes longer, until glazed and brown but not burned. Remove from grill and separate rack into individual ribs. Serve with remaining sauce on the side.

Serving (1 rib, with 1 tablespoon + 1 teaspoon sauce) provides: $^1/_4$ Vegetable, 1 $^1/_2$ Proteins, 15 Optional Calories.

Per serving: 154 Calories, 11 g Total Fat, 4 g Saturated Fat, 35 mg Cholesterol, 159 mg Sodium, 6 g Total Carbohydrate, 0 g Dietary Fiber, 8 g Protein, 16 mg Calcium.

MIDDLE EASTERN MEATBALL KABOBS WITH YOGURT SAUCE

Kabobs like these may seem exotic—they're traditional fare all over the Middle East—but they can be made easily with ingredients you have in your pantry.

Makes 4 servings

1 cup finely chopped onions
1 teaspoon salt
2 teaspoons ground cumin
8 ounces lean ground beef
 (10% or less fat)
$^1/_2$ ounce plain fresh bread crumbs
$^1/_4$ cup fresh parsley

1 tablespoon + 1 teaspoon minced
 fresh mint leaves
$^1/_2$ cup plain nonfat yogurt
1 teaspoon fresh lemon juice
$^1/_4$ teaspoon freshly ground
 black pepper

1. In small bowl, combine onions and $^3/_4$ teaspoon of the salt; set aside 30 minutes. Transfer to cheesecloth- or paper-towel-lined strainer; press firmly to squeeze out excess liquid.
2. Preheat grill for a medium fire, using direct method (see page xiii). If using wooden skewers, soak in water 30 minutes.
3. In small skillet, toast cumin over low heat 1 minute, just until fragrant; transfer to medium bowl. Add beef, bread crumbs, parsley and 2 teaspoons of the mint; mix well.
4. Divide mixture into 16 equal meatballs. Thread 4 balls onto each of four 12" metal or wooden skewers, squeezing meatballs gently to shape into oblongs.
5. In small bowl, combine yogurt, juice, the remaining mint and salt and the pepper.
6. Grill kabobs, turning once, until cooked through, about 6 minutes.
7. To serve, divide kabobs among 4 plates; serve with sauce.

Serving (1 kabob, with 2 tablespoons sauce) provides: $^1/_2$ Vegetable, 1 $^1/_2$ Proteins.

Per serving: 162 Calories, 8 g Total Fat, 8 g Saturated Fat, 38 mg Cholesterol, 627 mg Sodium, 8 g Total Carbohydrate, 1 g Dietary Fiber, 13 g Protein, 92 mg Calcium.

ITALIAN BURGERS

This version of Italian meatballs is so flavorful that you won't need ketchup, onions or other traditional burger toppings.

Makes 4 servings

Two 1-ounce slices white bread
15 ounces lean ground sirloin
   (10% or less fat)
¹/₃ cup finely minced flat-leaf
   parsley
2 tablespoons freshly grated
   Parmesan cheese

3 garlic cloves, minced
1 teaspoon dried basil
¹/₂ teaspoon freshly ground
   black pepper
¹/₄ teaspoon salt
Four 1-ounce hard rolls, split

1. Prepare grill for a medium fire, using direct method (see page xiii).
2. In a blender or food processor, pulse bread to a fine crumb.
3. In large bowl, combine beef, bread crumbs, parsley, cheese, garlic, basil, pepper and salt. Shape mixture into 4 equal patties.
4. Grill patties directly over coals, turning once, 10 minutes (medium) or 12 minutes (well-done). Serve each burger on a hard roll.

Serving (1 burger on roll) provides: 3 Proteins, 1 ¹/₂ Breads, 15 Optional Calories.

Per serving: 322 Calories, 13 g Total Fat, 5 g Saturated Fat, 68 mg Cholesterol, 485 mg Sodium, 24 g Total Carbohydrate, 1 g Dietary Fiber, 27 g Protein, 95 mg Calcium.

BARBECUED BEEF AND LENTIL BURGERS

Lentils make a terrific, high-fiber "stretcher" for ground beef—plus they taste great!

Makes 4 servings

10 ounces lean ground beef
(10% or less fat)
4 ounces drained cooked lentils
1/4 cup finely chopped onion
1/4 cup barbecue sauce
1 tablespoon minced fresh
parsley

4 slices low-fat process American
cheese
Four 2-ounce hamburger rolls,
split and grilled
1 medium tomato, sliced

1. Preheat grill for a medium fire, using direct method (see page xiii).
2. In large bowl, combine beef, lentils, onion, barbecue sauce and parsley. Shape mixture into 4 equal patties.
3. Grill, turning once, 10 minutes or until done to taste. Place 1 slice of cheese on each patty; grill just until cheese melts. Serve each burger on a roll with sliced tomato.

Serving (1 burger on roll, with cheese and tomato) provides: 1/2 Vegetable, 3 Proteins, 2 Breads, 20 Optional Calories.

Per serving: 408 Calories, 15 g Total Fat, 6 g Saturated Fat, 54 mg Cholesterol, 763 mg Sodium, 40 g Total Carbohydrate, 3 g Dietary Fiber, 26 g Protein, 232 mg Calcium.

KANSAS CITY BARBECUED BEEF ON A BUN

A tomato-y, vinegary sauce with a just a hint of sweetness: that's what makes Kansas City barbecue special.

Makes 6 servings

2 tablespoons red wine vinegar	$^1/_2$ cup grated onion
1 tablespoon vegetable oil	$^1/_4$ cup ketchup
1 teaspoon paprika	2 teaspoons dark molasses
1 garlic clove, minced	1 teaspoon chili powder
One 1-pound 8-ounce trimmed flank steak	1 teaspoon steak sauce
	Six 1-ounce hard rolls

1. Combine vinegar, 2 teaspoons of the oil, the paprika and garlic; add steak and marinate at least 6 hours or overnight (see page xvi). Transfer steak to a platter and drizzle with any remaining marinade.
2. Prepare grill for a medium-hot fire, using direct method (see page xiii).
3. Meanwhile, prepare barbecue sauce. In small bowl, combine onion, ketchup, molasses, chili powder, steak sauce and the remaining teaspoon oil; set aside 2 tablespoons of mixture and spread the rest onto both sides of steak.
4. Grill steak, turning once, 10 minutes (medium) or 12 minutes (well-done). Transfer to platter and cover with foil; let stand 10 minutes. Thinly slice and serve on rolls, each with a teaspoon of reserved barbecue sauce.

Serving (3 ounces beef, on roll, and 1 teaspoon barbecue sauce) provides: $^1/_2$ Fat, 3 Proteins, 1 Bread, 15 Optional Calories.

Per serving: 307 Calories, 12 g Total Fat, 4 g Saturated Fat, 57 mg Cholesterol, 366 mg Sodium, 21 g Total Carbohydrate, 1 g Dietary Fiber, 26 g Protein, 63 mg Calcium.

LONE STAR BRISKET SANDWICHES

Brisket can be tough if it's not treated right. Overnight marinating and long, slow cooking suit it best; a smoker is ideal, but a covered grill works fine with our method.

Makes 6 servings

2/3 cup cider vinegar
2 teaspoons ground
   red pepper
2 teaspoons steak sauce
One 1-pound 8-ounce
   trimmed beef brisket
2 tablespoons paprika

2 teaspoons onion powder
1 teaspoon chili powder
1 teaspoon garlic powder
1 teaspoon granulated sugar
$^1/_2$ teaspoon ground cloves
Six 1-ounce hard rolls

1. Combine vinegar, pepper and steak sauce; reserve, cover and refrigerate $^1/_2$ cup of mixture for "mop" sauce. Add steak to remaining mixture and marinate 6–8 hours or overnight (see page xvi).
2. In small bowl, combine paprika, onion powder, chili powder, garlic powder, sugar and cloves; set aside.
3. Remove steak with tongs, shaking off excess marinade; pat brisket dry with paper towels; place on plate. Discard any remaining marinade. Spread spice mixture evenly over steak, rubbing into meat. Cover with plastic wrap; refrigerate 4 hours. Remove and let stand at room temperature 30 minutes.
4. Soak 2–3 handfuls hickory or mesquite wood chips in water 1 hour; drain. Prepare grill for a low, long-burning fire, using indirect method (see page xiii).

5. Sprinkle drained wood chips onto coals and grill brisket until well browned on both sides, about 10 minutes. Cover grill and continue cooking 10 minutes. Turn meat and baste with 1 tablespoon reserved "mop" sauce; cook 10 minutes more. Remove meat and wrap in double layer of heavy foil, leaving an opening in top of foil. Pour remaining "mop" sauce through opening; return packet to grill, cover and continue cooking until meat is very tender, 2–2 1/2 hours, basting meat occasionally with "mop" sauce at bottom of foil packet and replenishing wood chips and coals as needed. Remove packet and let stand 10 minutes; cut into thin slices or, if you prefer "pulled" barbecue, flake meat into strands with fork. Divide evenly among 6 rolls and serve.

Serving (3 ounces beef on roll) provides: 3 Proteins, 1 Bread, 3 Optional Calories.

Per serving: 313 Calories, 13 g Total Fat, 4 g Saturated Fat, 79 mg Cholesterol, 238 mg Sodium, 20 g Total Carbohydrate, 1 g Dietary Fiber, 29 g Protein, 44 mg Calcium.

GAUCHO BRISKET

Loosely adapted from the Argentine Asado, this spicy beef is served with a tangy sauce that enhances its richness. Any leftovers are delicious cold.

Makes 24 servings

One 4-pound trimmed
  beef brisket
1 cup finely chopped onions
6–8 garlic cloves, finely minced
2 teaspoons coarsely ground
  black pepper

$^1/_2$–2 teaspoons ground
  red pepper
1 tablespoon + 2 teaspoons
  unseasoned meat tenderizer
1 $^1/_2$ cups Argentine Green Sauce
  (page 149)

1. With sharp knife, pierce brisket at 2" intervals, making slits 1" deep. In small bowl, combine onions, garlic and black and red peppers. Pack mixture into slits, rubbing any extra over meat. Wrap brisket in plastic wrap and refrigerate overnight.
2. Prepare grill for a low fire, using indirect method (see page xiii). When coals are ready, place drip pan on grate and half fill with water. Set grill in place.
3. Meanwhile, moisten brisket with water. Sprinkle evenly on all sides with meat tenderizer and pierce at 1" intervals with fork; let stand 30 minutes. Wrap in heavy-duty foil and place on grill. Cover, with bottom vent open and top vent half open, and grill for 2 hours, adding 5 lighted briquets to each side of coals every hour.
4. Remove packet from grill. Holding packet over bowl, drain out any juices. Remove and discard foil; return meat to grill. Baste meat with juices. Cover and continue grilling 1 hour longer, basting twice. Remove to serving platter or carving board, cover loosely with foil, and let stand 15 minutes. Slice thinly across the grain and serve with Argentine Green Sauce.

Serving (2 ounces brisket, with 1 tablespoon sauce) provides: 3 Proteins, 8 Optional Calories.

Per serving: 148 Calories, 8 g Total Fat, 3 g Saturated Fat, 53 mg Cholesterol, 423 mg Sodium, 1 g Total Carbohydrate, 0 g Dietary Fiber, 17 g Protein, 88 mg Calcium.

5

VEGETABLES

Grilled Stuffed Onions • Grilled Stuffed Acorn Squash

Rice-and-Vegetable Stuffed Grilled Zucchini • Grilled Baby Artichokes

Grilled Endive • Grilled Tomatoes • Grilled Cucumbers

Grilled Radicchio Vinaigrette • Grilled Leeks Vinaigrette • Grilled Portobello
Mushrooms in Madeira Marinade

Grilled Eggplant and Tomato with Basil • Glazed Carrots in Foil

Green Beans in Foil • Foil-Wrapped Greens

Herbed Beets in Foil • Wilted Coleslaw

Grilled Eggplant–Potato Moussaka • Grilled Vegetable Tian • Grilled Ratatouille

GRILLED STUFFED ONIONS

Use the sweetest onions you can find—such as Vidalia, Maui or Walla Walla onions—for this delicious side dish.

Makes 4 servings

4 medium onions
2 teaspoons reduced-calorie
    tub margarine
1 cup diced celery
$^1/_2$ cup diced fennel
$^1/_4$ teaspoon salt

$^1/_8$ teaspoon freshly ground
    black pepper
$^1/_2$ cup chopped kale
1 tablespoon + 1 teaspoon plain
    dried bread crumbs

1. Prepare grill for a medium fire, using direct method (see page xiii).
2. Slice $^1/_2$" off top of each onion; scoop out center, leaving 3 outer layers of shell. Be careful not to cut through bottom root. Dice tops and centers and set aside.
3. Place medium saucepan over low heat 30 seconds; melt margarine 30 seconds more. Add diced onions, the celery, fennel, salt and pepper; cook, stirring frequently, 12 minutes. Add kale and cook another 4 minutes, until vegetables are wilted and soft. Set aside.
4. Spray onion shells lightly with nonstick cooking spray; grill shells, hollowside down, turning frequently, 7–10 minutes, until they begin to soften.
5. Spoon one-fourth of the stuffing into cavity of each onion. Top each with 1 teaspoon of the bread crumbs. Place stuffed onions on grill over medium-low heat and cook, 30 minutes, until golden brown. Transfer onions to each of 4 plates and serve.

Serving (1 stuffed onion) provides: $^1/_4$ Fat, 2 Vegetables, 10 Optional Calories.

Per serving: 68 Calories, 2 g Total Fat, 0 g Saturated Fat, 0 mg Cholesterol, 217 mg Sodium, 11 g Total Carbohydrate, 3 g Dietary Fiber, 2 g Protein, 53 mg Calcium.

GRILLED STUFFED ACORN SQUASH

Acorn squash is an old favorite made new by the flavor of grilling.

Makes 4 servings

2 teaspoons reduced-calorie
   tub margarine
³/₄ cup diced onions
1¹/₂ cups diced apples

³/₄ cup diced celery
¹/₄ cup golden raisins
Two 15-ounce acorn squashes,
   rinsed, halved and seeded

1. Prepare grill for a low fire, using direct method (see page xiii).
2. To prepare filling, place medium saucepan over medium heat 30 seconds; melt margarine 30 seconds more. Add onions; cook, stirring constantly, 3 minutes. Add apples, celery and raisins; cook, stirring frequently, 6 minutes, until soft. Set aside.
3. Grill squashes, cut-side down, 10 minutes.
4. Divide filling evenly among squash halves. Grill, covered, 40 minutes, until soft and lightly browned. Transfer squash halves to each of 4 plates and serve.

Serving (one-half stuffed squash) provides: ¹/₄ Fat, 1¹/₄ Fruits,
³/₄ Vegetable, 1 Bread.

Per serving: 140 Calories, 1 g Total Fat, 0 g Saturated Fat, 0 mg Cholesterol, 43 mg Sodium, 34 g Total Carbohydrate, 8 g Dietary Fiber, 2 g Protein, 76 mg Calcium.

RICE-AND-VEGETABLE STUFFED GRILLED ZUCCHINI

Sliced into bite-size, sushi-like rounds, this stuffed zucchini is especially pretty.

Makes 4 servings

2 medium zucchini
(8 ounces each)
1 teaspoon extra virgin olive oil
$1/2$ cup chopped onion
$1/2$ cup chopped plum tomatoes
2 medium garlic cloves, minced
$1/2$ cup cooked white rice, cooled

6 large kalamata olives, pitted and
chopped
$1/8$ teaspoon freshly ground
black pepper
3 tablespoons minced fresh basil
2 teaspoons freshly grated
Parmesan cheese

1. Preheat grill for a medium fire, using direct method (see page xiii). Spray grill rack with nonstick cooking spray.
2. Trim ends from each zucchini; cut zucchini in half horizontally. With sharp paring knife, cut a hole lengthwise through each zucchini half: insert knife tip and turn it until inner flesh loosens. Remove inner flesh, hollowing out zucchini from end to end to form a tube. Chop inner flesh and set aside.
3. Place medium nonstick skillet over medium heat 30 seconds; heat oil 30 seconds more. Add onion and cook, stirring constantly, until translucent, 6–8 minutes. Add reserved chopped zucchini, the tomatoes and garlic; cook, stirring, 1 minute. Stir in rice, olives and pepper; cook 1 minute more. Remove from heat; stir in basil and Parmesan cheese. Let cool slightly. With fingers, stuff one-fourth of mixture tightly into each zucchini cavity.
4. Place stuffed zucchini halves on prepared rack and grill, turning occasionally, until well-browned and heated through, about 20 minutes. Slice each zucchini half into $1/2$" rounds. Divide evenly among 4 plates and serve.

Serving ($1/2$ stuffed zucchini) provides: $1/2$ Fat, $1 1/2$ Vegetables, $1/4$ Bread, 5 Optional Calories.

Per serving: 102 Calories, 4 g Total Fat, 1 g Saturated Fat, 1 mg Cholesterol, 255 mg Sodium, 15 g Total Carbohydrate, 1 g Dietary Fiber, 3 g Protein, 61 mg Calcium.

GRILLED BABY ARTICHOKES

Artichokes may seem like unlikely candidates for the grill, but baby ones—about the size of large walnuts—are perfect when grilled to a crispy brown. Eat them whole, leaves and all!

Makes 4 servings

1 pound 2 ounces baby
   artichokes, rinsed
$^1/_2$ lemon
6–8 cups ice water
$^1/_4$ cup fresh lemon juice

2 garlic cloves, minced
$^1/_4$ teaspoon salt
$^1/_4$ teaspoon freshly ground
   black pepper

1. Prepare grill for a medium fire, using direct method (see page xiii).
2. Trim $^1/_8$" off tops and bottoms of artichokes and remove any loose or discolored leaves. Slice artichokes in half lengthwise through the heart. Rub each half with cut side of lemon.
3. Bring large saucepan of water to a boil; drop in artichokes and cook 1 minute. With slotted spoon, transfer to large bowl of ice water to stop cooking; drain when completely cooled.
4. In medium bowl, combine cooked artichokes, lemon juice, garlic, salt and pepper; toss well.
5. Spray grill basket with nonstick cooking spray. Place as many artichokes as will fit in single layer in grill basket. Grill over medium heat, about 9 minutes per side, until crispy brown and tender. Transfer cooked artichokes to platter; cover with foil to keep warm. Repeat with remaining artichokes. Divide evenly among 4 plates and serve.

Serving (about 1 cup) provides: 1 Vegetable.

Per serving: 38 Calories, 0 g Total Fat, 0 g Saturated Fat, 0 mg Cholesterol, 179 mg Sodium, 8 g Total Carbohydrate, 3 g Dietary Fiber, 2 g Protein, 22 mg Calcium.

GRILLED ENDIVE

If this slightly bitter vegetable is new to you, grilling is a marvelous introduction. It can be prepared and marinated ahead and grilled quickly at the last minute; be careful not to char the delicate leaves.

Makes 4 servings

4 medium heads Belgian endive,
  halved lengthwise,
  washed and drained

2 tablespoons fresh lemon juice
1 tablespoon olive oil
Pinch freshly ground black pepper

1. Prepare grill for a medium fire, using direct method (see page xiii).
2. In medium nonreactive bowl, combine endive, juice, oil and pepper, tossing gently to coat. Cover and let stand 1–4 hours, tossing occasionally.
3. Just before serving, remove endive from marinade with tongs and place along edges of grill. Grill 3 minutes; turn and grill 3 minutes longer; do not char. Drizzle with any remaining marinade, divide evenly among 4 plates and serve.

Serving (2 endive halves) provides: ³/₄ Fat, 1 Vegetable.

Per serving: 47 Calories, 3 g Total Fat, 0 g Saturated Fat, 0 mg Cholesterol, 9 mg Sodium, 4 g Total Carbohydrate, 2 g Dietary Fiber, 1 g Protein, 1 mg Calcium.

GRILLED TOMATOES

The wonderful thing about grilling tomatoes is that it makes even winter tomatoes taste good. Plum tomatoes are even better, and, of course, firm vine-
ripened summer tomatoes are sheer heaven.

Makes 4 servings

8–10 medium garlic cloves,
minced
1 tablespoon minced fresh basil
or 1 teaspoon dried basil,
oregano or thyme

1 tablespoon olive oil
Pinch salt
4 medium beefsteak tomatoes,
or 8 large plum tomatoes,
halved lengthwise

1. In small bowl, combine garlic, basil, oil and salt.
2. If using beefsteak tomatoes, cut stems out to make a $^1/_2$" cavity, then cut thin
slice from bottoms so they will stand level on grill. Fill each cavity with one-
fourth of the garlic mixture. If using plum tomatoes, halve lengthwise, then
spoon garlic mixture evenly onto cut sides. Let stand at room temperature
1 hour.
3. Prepare grill for a medium fire, using direct method (see page xiii).
4. Grill beefsteak tomatoes along edges of grill about 15–20 minutes, until hot.
If using plum tomatoes, thread onto four 12" metal skewers and grill along
edges of grill about 5 minutes, until hot. Serve hot or at room temperature.

Serving (1 beefsteak tomato or 4 plum tomato halves) provides: $^3/_4$ Fat,
2 Vegetables.

Per serving: 57 Calories, 4 g Total Fat, 1 g Saturated Fat, 0 mg Cholesterol,
43 mg Sodium, 6 g Total Carbohydrate, 1 g Dietary Fiber, 1 g Protein,
14 mg Calcium.

GRILLED CUCUMBERS

Cucumber tastes like an entirely different vegetable when it's cooked. Served warm, it's an excellent side dish with salmon or lamb; chilled, it goes well with cold meat, fish or poultry.

Makes 4 servings

$^1/_2$ cup very thinly sliced onion

3 tablespoons white wine vinegar

2 teaspoons minced fresh dill (optional)

1 large garlic clove, peeled and bruised

$^1/_2$ teaspoon granulated sugar

$^1/_4$ teaspoon salt

$^1/_4$ teaspoon freshly ground black pepper

2 medium cucumbers, pared, quartered lengthwise and seeded

1. In large bowl, combine onion, vinegar, dill (if using), garlic, sugar, salt and pepper. Let stand at least 1 hour to blend flavors; remove and discard garlic.
2. Prepare grill for a medium fire, using direct method (see page xiii).
3. Place cucumber wedges along edges of grill; grill 3–5 minutes, turning often, just to heat through. Transfer to large bowl; toss immediately with vinegar mixture and serve warm, or cover and refrigerate until chilled. Divide evenly among 4 plates and serve.

Serving ($^1/_2$ cucumber, with 1 tablespoon dressing) provides: 1 $^1/_4$ Vegetables, 2 Optional Calories.

Per serving: 20 Calories, 0 g Total Fat, 0 g Saturated Fat, 0 mg Cholesterol, 139 mg Sodium, 5 g Total Carbohydrate, 1 g Dietary Fiber, 1 g Protein, 15 mg Calcium.

GRILLED RADICCHIO VINAIGRETTE

Grilling mellows the slightly bitter flavor of radicchio; fresh basil vinaigrette brightens it. This is an elegant side dish for a festive dinner *al fresco*.

Makes 4 servings

2 heads radicchio (4 ounces each), trimmed and quartered

$^1/_4$ cup + 2 tablespoons minced fresh basil

1 tablespoon + 1 teaspoon balsamic vinegar

2 teaspoons extra virgin olive oil

$^1/_4$ teaspoon salt

$^1/_8$ teaspoon freshly ground black pepper

1. Preheat grill for a medium fire, using direct method (see page xiii). Spray grill rack with nonstick cooking spray.
2. Place radicchio quarters on prepared rack and grill, turning once, until just cooked through, about 8 minutes.
3. Meanwhile, in small bowl, combine basil, 2 tablespoons water, the vinegar, oil, salt and pepper.
4. Put 2 quarters on each of 4 plates, drizzle evenly with vinaigrette and serve.

Serving (2 radicchio quarters, with one-fourth of vinaigrette) provides:
$^1/_2$ Fat, 1 Vegetable.

Per serving: 33 Calories, 3 g Total Fat, 0 g Saturated Fat, 0 mg Cholesterol, 140 mg Sodium, 3 g Total Carbohydrate, 0 g Dietary Fiber, 1 g Protein, 66 mg Calcium.

GRILLED LEEKS VINAIGRETTE

Leeks, with their subtle flavor, make an excellent side dish for grilled fish or chicken.

Makes 4 servings

4 medium leeks, trimmed
and well-washed
2 tablespoons minced
fresh parsley
2 tablespoons white wine vinegar
1 tablespoon olive oil
$^1/_2$ teaspoon minced fresh
thyme leaves

$^1/_2$ teaspoon grated orange zest*
$^1/_2$ teaspoon Dijon-style mustard
$^1/_4$ teaspoon salt
$^1/_8$ teaspoon freshly ground
black pepper

1. With sharp knife, slit white part of leeks lengthwise toward root end just up to light green part; do not cut all the way through. Soak in cold water 1 hour to release grit.
2. Prepare grill for a medium fire, using direct method (see page xiii).
3. To prepare vinaigrette, in small bowl, combine parsley, vinegar, oil, 1 teaspoon water, the thyme, zest, mustard, salt and pepper. Set aside.
4. Place leeks in medium saucepan; cover with 2" water. Cover and bring to a boil; reduce heat to low and cook 5 minutes, until tender. Rinse in colander under cold running water and drain on paper towels. Finish cutting through lengthwise.
5. Grill leeks 8–10 minutes, turning once, until lightly browned. Put 2 halves on each of 4 plates, drizzle evenly with vinaigrette and serve.

Serving (1 leek, with 1 tablespoon vinaigrette) provides: $^3/_4$ Fat,
1 Vegetable.

Per serving: 93 Calories, 4 g Total Fat, 0 g Saturated Fat, 0 mg Cholesterol, 171 mg Sodium, 15 g Total Carbohydrate, 1 g Dietary Fiber, 2 g Protein, 64 mg Calcium.

*The zest of the orange is the peel without any of the pith (white membrane). To remove zest from orange, use a zester or vegetable peeler. To grate zest, use a zester or fine side of a vegetable grater; wrap in plastic and refrigerate for later use.

GRILLED PORTOBELLO MUSHROOMS IN MADEIRA MARINADE

This is also a terrific appetizer served plain or on a small round of sourdough bread.

Makes 4 servings

2 fluid ounces (¹/₄ cup) Madeira wine
1 tablespoon balsamic vinegar
1 tablespoon extra virgin olive oil
1 tablespoon light tamari or reduced-sodium soy sauce
1 garlic clove, minced
1 tablespoon minced fresh oregano (or 1 teaspoon dried)

1 tablespoon minced fresh basil (or 1 teaspoon dried)
1 tablespoon minced fresh parsley (or 1 teaspoon dried)
12 ounces portobello mushroom caps

1. Combine wine, vinegar, oil, tamari or soy sauce, garlic, oregano, basil and parsley; add mushrooms and marinate at least 6 hours or overnight (see page xvi).
2. Prepare grill for a medium fire, using direct method (see page xiii).
3. Drain marinade into small saucepan. Bring to a rolling boil; boil for one minute, stirring constantly. Remove from heat.
4. Meanwhile, grill mushrooms, stemmed-side down, turning occasionally, until golden brown on both sides, about 7 minutes. Transfer to a serving platter and pour marinade evenly over mushrooms. Divide evenly among 4 plates and serve.

Serving (³/₄ cup mushrooms, with marinade) provides: ³/₄ Fat, 1 ¹/₂ Vegetables, 25 Optional Calories.

Per serving: 69 Calories, 4 g Total Fat, 1 g Saturated Fat, 0 mg Cholesterol, 154 mg Sodium, 5 g Total Carbohydrate, 1 g Dietary Fiber, 2 g Protein, 11 mg Calcium.

GRILLED EGGPLANT AND TOMATO WITH BASIL

The meaty flavor of eggplant is perfect for grilling; served with rice or pasta, this makes a wonderful meal.

Makes 4 servings

$^1/_2$ cup diced yellow bell pepper
$^1/_4$ cup low-sodium chicken broth
1 tablespoon + 1 teaspoon olive oil
1 tablespoon balsamic vinegar
2 garlic cloves, minced
$^1/_4$ teaspoon salt
$^1/_4$ teaspoon freshly ground
   black pepper

1 medium eggplant, pared and
   cut into 1" slices
1 medium tomato, cut into
   $^1/_2$" slices
3 ounces goat cheese, crumbled
$^1/_4$ cup coarsely chopped basil

1. In mini food processor or blender, purée bell pepper, broth, oil, vinegar, garlic, salt and black pepper until smooth. Place eggplant and tomato on plate and brush on both sides with broth mixture; discard any remaining broth mixture.
2. Prepare grill for a medium fire, using direct method (see page xiii).
3. Grill eggplant 8 minutes, turning after 4 minutes, until lightly charred. Grill tomatoes 4 minutes, turning after 2 minutes.
4. Arrange eggplant and tomato alternately on platter, overlapping slices. Sprinkle cheese and scatter basil evenly over all. Divide evenly among 4 plates and serve.

Serving (1 cup) provides: 1 Fat, 1$^3/_4$ Vegetables, 1 Protein, 1 Optional Calorie.

Per serving: 161 Calories, 11 g Total Fat, 5 g Saturated Fat, 17 mg Cholesterol, 260 mg Sodium, 11 g Total Carbohydrate, 2 g Dietary Fiber, 7 g Protein, 124 mg Calcium.

GLAZED CARROTS IN FOIL

These carrots have a rich roasted flavor, with nary a pan to clean!

Makes 4 servings

4 cups diagonally sliced carrots
8 garlic cloves, peeled and halved
2 teaspoons olive oil

$^1/_4$ teaspoon salt
$^1/_4$ teaspoon freshly ground
black pepper

1. Prepare grill for a medium fire, using direct method (see page xiii).
2. In medium bowl, combine carrots, garlic, 1 tablespoon water, the oil, salt and pepper. Transfer to center of double layer of heavy-duty, extra-wide foil. Make packet by bringing 2 sides of foil up to meet in center and pressing edges together in two $^1/_2$" folds. Then fold edges of each end together in two $^1/_2$" folds. Allowing room for packet to expand, crimp edges together to seal.
3. Grill carrots 25 minutes, until cooked through. Remove from grill and open packet carefully, as hot steam will escape. Divide evenly among 4 plates and serve.

Serving ($^3/_4$ cup) provides: $^1/_2$ Fat, 2 Vegetables.

Per serving: 76 Calories, 2 g Total Fat, 0 g Saturated Fat, 0 mg Cholesterol, 175 mg Sodium, 13 g Total Carbohydrate, 4 g Dietary Fiber, 2 g Protein, 42 mg Calcium.

GREEN BEANS IN FOIL

Try making these beans a day ahead–they make a great cold salad.

Makes 4 servings

2 cups trimmed green beans

1 tablespoon minced fresh mint leaves

1 tablespoon fresh lemon juice

2 teaspoons olive oil

$^1/_4$ teaspoon salt

$^1/_8$ teaspoon freshly ground black pepper

1. Prepare grill for a medium fire, using direct method (see page xiii).
2. In medium bowl, combine beans, mint, juice, oil, salt and pepper. Transfer to center of double layer of heavy-duty, extra-wide aluminum foil. Make packet by bringing 2 sides of foil up to meet in center, and pressing edges together in two $^1/_2$" folds. Then fold edges of each end together in two $^1/_2$" folds. Allowing room for packet to expand, crimp edges together to seal.
3. Grill beans 15 minutes, until cooked through. Remove from grill and open packet carefully, as hot steam will escape. Divide evenly among 4 plates and serve.

Serving ($^1/_2$ cup) provides: $^1/_2$ Fat, 1 Vegetable.

Per serving: 38 Calories, 2 g Total Fat, 0 g Saturated Fat, 0 mg Cholesterol, 139 mg Sodium, 4 g Total Carbohydrate, 1 g Dietary Fiber, 1 g Protein, 22 mg Calcium.

FOIL-WRAPPED GREENS

Greens on the grill? Yes, this inventive way of cooking greens gives them flavor while steaming them ever so gently.

Makes 4 servings

4 cups tightly packed washed
   trimmed greens, such as kale,
   dandelion greens or spinach
1 tablespoon olive oil
1 tablespoon balsamic vinegar

2 medium garlic cloves, minced
$^{1}/_{4}$ teaspoon salt
$^{1}/_{4}$ teaspoon freshly ground
   black pepper

1. Prepare grill for a medium fire, using direct method (see page xiii).
2. In medium bowl, combine greens, 2 tablespoons water, the oil, vinegar, garlic, salt and pepper. Transfer to center of double layer of heavy-duty foil. Make packet by bringing 2 sides of foil up to meet in center and pressing edges together in two $^{1}/_{2}$" folds. Then fold edges of each end together in two $^{1}/_{2}$" folds. Allowing room for packet to expand, crimp edges together to seal.
3. Grill greens 10–12 minutes, until cooked through. Remove from grill and open packet carefully, as hot steam will escape. Divide evenly among 4 plates and serve.

Serving ($^{1}/_{2}$ cup) provides: $^{3}/_{4}$ Fat, 2 Vegetables

Per serving: 100 Calories, 4 g Total Fat, 1 g Saturated Fat, 0 mg Cholesterol, 194 mg Sodium, 14 g Total Carbohydrate, 9 g Dietary Fiber, 5 g Protein, 187 mg Calcium.

HERBED BEETS IN FOIL

Roasting beets this way brings out their natural sweetness while giving them a subtle herb flavor.

Makes 4 servings

2 teaspoons minced fresh
   thyme leaves
2 teaspoons olive oil
1/4 teaspoon salt

1/4 teaspoon freshly ground
   black pepper
4 pared trimmed beets
   (about 12 ounces)

1. Prepare grill for a medium fire, using direct method (see page xiii).
2. In small bowl, combine thyme, oil, salt and pepper. Place 1 beet in center of large piece heavy-duty foil; drizzle one-fourth of thyme mixture over beet. Make packet by bringing 2 sides of foil up to meet in center and pressing edges together in two 1/2" folds. Then fold edges of each end together in two 1/2" folds. Allowing room for packet to expand, crimp edges together to seal. Repeat with remaining beets and herb mixture.
3. Grill beets 40 minutes, until cooked through. Remove from grill and open each packet carefully, as hot steam will escape. Transfer contents to 4 plates and serve.

Serving (1 beet) provides: 1/2 Fat, 1 Vegetable.

Per serving: 47 Calories, 2 g Total Fat, 0 g Saturated Fat, 0 mg Cholesterol, 178 mg Sodium, 6 g Total Carbohydrate, 1 g Dietary Fiber, 1 g Protein, 14 mg Calcium.

WILTED COLESLAW

This recipe is an unusual twist on traditional coleslaw. The flavors are similar, but it is made without mayonnaise for a lighter consistency and a fresher taste.

Makes 4 servings

1 ½ cups shredded green cabbage
1 cup shredded carrots
½ cup slivered red bell pepper
½ cup slivered red onion
2 teaspoons olive oil

2 teaspoons white wine vinegar
1 teaspoon granulated sugar
¼ teaspoon celery seeds
¼ teaspoon salt

1. Prepare grill for a medium fire, using direct method (see page xiii).
2. In medium bowl, combine cabbage, carrots, pepper, onion, oil, vinegar, sugar, celery seeds and salt. Transfer to center of double layer of heavy-duty, extra-wide foil. Make packet by bringing 2 sides of foil up to meet in center and pressing edges together in two ½" folds. Then fold edges of each end together in two ½" folds. Allowing room for packet to expand, crimp edges together to seal.
3. Grill vegetables 15–18 minutes, until cooked through. Remove from grill and open packet carefully, as hot steam will escape. Divide evenly among 4 plates and serve.

Serving (½ cup) provides: ½ Fat, 1 ¾ Vegetables, 4 Optional Calories.

Per serving: 54 Calories, 2 g Total Fat, 0 g Saturated Fat, 0 mg Cholesterol, 152 mg Sodium, 8 g Total Carbohydrate, 2 g Dietary Fiber, 1 g Protein, 30 mg Calcium.

GRILLED EGGPLANT—POTATO MOUSSAKA

Moussaka, a traditional Greek specialty, makes a great one-dish meal. This vegetable version is light and delicious. Make it the day ahead and reheat gently or serve at room temperature.

Makes 4 servings

1 medium eggplant, cut into
  $1/4$" slices
1 pound 4 ounces all-purpose
  potatoes, pared and quartered
1 cup low-fat (1%) milk
$3/4$ teaspoon salt
$3/4$ teaspoon freshly ground
  black pepper
1 teaspoon olive oil
$1/2$ cup diced onion
2 cups diced drained canned
  tomatoes

1 tablespoon red wine vinegar
1 teaspoon dried oregano
4 garlic cloves, minced
1 cup finely shredded kale
$1/4$ cup low-sodium chicken broth
2 teaspoons arrowroot* mixed with
  2 teaspoons water
$1/4$ teaspoon freshly grated nutmeg
2 teaspoons freshly grated
  Parmesan cheese
$1/4$ cup minced fresh flat-leaf
  parsley

1. Prepare grill for a medium fire, using direct method (see page xiii); spray grill basket lightly with nonstick cooking spray.
2. Grill eggplant slices in prepared grill basket, 2 minutes per side, until golden brown and tender. Set aside.
3. Place potatoes in medium saucepan and cover with 2" water. Bring to a boil over medium-high heat; reduce heat to medium and simmer 15 minutes, until tender. Drain and return to pot. With electric beater or hand masher, coarsely mash potatoes; add $1/4$ cup of the milk and $1/2$ teaspoon each of the salt and pepper. Continue mashing until smooth and free of most lumps. Set aside.
4. Place small saucepan over medium-high heat 30 seconds; heat oil 30 seconds more. Add onion and cook, stirring constantly, 2 minutes. Add tomatoes, vinegar, oregano and garlic; cook over medium heat, stirring frequently, 7 minutes. Set aside.
5. Preheat oven to 350° F. Spray 1-quart baking dish with nonstick cooking spray. Place one-third of the grilled eggplant slices in single layer on bottom of dish, top with one-half of the mashed potatoes; sprinkle one-half of the kale evenly over potatoes, top with one-half of the tomato mixture. Repeat layering, ending with eggplant slices; set aside.

6. In small saucepan, bring the remaining ³/₄ cup milk and the broth almost to a boil; whisk in arrowroot mixture, nutmeg, the remaining ¹/₄ teaspoon each salt and pepper; simmer, whisking constantly, 2 minutes, until thick. Remove from heat.

7. Pour thickened milk mixture over vegetables and spread as evenly as possible with back of spoon; top with Parmesan cheese. Bake 45 minutes, until bubbling and browned. Divide evenly among 4 plates, sprinkle with parsley and serve.

Serving (1 ¹/₂ cups) provides: ¹/₄ Milk, ¹/₄ Fat, 3 ¹/₄ Vegetables, 1 Bread, 10 Optional Calories.

Per serving: 225 Calories, 3 g Total Fat, 1 g Saturated Fat, 3 mg Cholesterol, 684 mg Sodium, 43 g Total Carbohydrate, 6 g Dietary Fiber, 8 g Protein, 186 mg Calcium.

*Arrowroot is a fine powdered starch used for thickening. It is mixed with cold liquid to form a paste before being stirred into hot mixtures. If unavailable, substitute an equal amount of cornstarch or potato starch or substitute 1 tablespoon + 1 teaspoon flour. If using flour, add 10 Optional Calories per serving.

GRILLED VEGETABLE TIAN

Alternating layers of vegetables in a shallow dish make an attractive, brightly colored presentation.

Makes 4 servings

2 medium red bell peppers,
  quartered
1 medium eggplant, thinly sliced
8 medium scallions, trimmed
2 tablespoons red wine vinegar
1 tablespoon olive oil

Pinch dried oregano
Pinch dried basil
Pinch salt
Freshly ground black pepper,
  to taste

1. Prepare grill for a medium fire, using direct method (see page xiii).
2. Grill peppers 10 minutes, turning once, until slightly charred and fork-tender. Grill eggplant 5 minutes, turning once, until slightly charred and fork-tender. Grill scallions about 3 minutes, until slightly charred and fork-tender.
3. In small bowl, whisk together vinegar, oil, 1 tablespoon water, the oregano, basil, salt and pepper.
4. Cut scallions into 2" pieces. In wide, shallow serving dish, alternate layers of eggplant, peppers and scallions, drizzling small amount of vinaigrette over each layer. Pour remaining dressing over top. Cover and chill at least 1 hour to blend flavors. Divide evenly among 4 plates and serve at room temperature or slightly chilled.

Serving (¹/₂ cup) provides: ³/₄ Fat, 2³/₄ Vegetables.

Per serving: 81 Calories, 4 g Total Fat, 0 g Saturated Fat, 0 mg Cholesterol, 41 mg Sodium, 12 g Total Carbohydrate, 3 g Dietary Fiber, 2 g Protein, 62 mg Calcium.

GRILLED RATATOUILLE

This mélange of summer vegetables receives an irresistibly earthy, smoky flavor from the grill. Make it a day ahead if you like; serve it cold, hot or at room temperature. Leftovers make a wonderful pasta sauce, or a superb filling for an omelet or a sandwich. Make it often to keep some on hand all summer long.

Makes 8 servings

2 tablespoons + 2 teaspoons
  fruity olive oil
2–4 tablespoons slivered fresh basil
1 tablespoon red wine vinegar
$^1/_2$ teaspoon salt
$^1/_2$ teaspoon freshly ground
  black pepper
2 large onions, peeled
  (do not cut root end) and
  quartered
4 small (6") zucchini, scrubbed
  and cut into 1" chunks

12 large plum tomatoes, halved
  lengthwise
1 medium eggplant, pared and
  cut into 1" cubes
1 medium red bell pepper, seeded
  and cut into eighths
1 medium green bell pepper, seeded
  and cut into eighths
1 head Roasted Garlic (page 159)

1. Prepare grill for a medium-hot fire, using direct method (see page xiii). If using wooden skewers, soak in water 30 minutes.
2. In large bowl, combine oil, basil, vinegar, salt and pepper; set aside.
3. Thread onions, zucchini, tomatoes, eggplant and bell peppers separately onto twelve 12" metal or wooden skewers (approximately 2 skewers per vegetable). Grill directly over coals, turning frequently, until very lightly charred, about 12 minutes for the onions, 8–10 minutes for the tomatoes and peppers and about 6 minutes for the zucchini and eggplant. As vegetables are done, slide them off skewers and into bowl with vinaigrette, tossing lightly after each addition.
4. Cut top off Roasted Garlic and squeeze pulp out of papery skins onto grilled vegetables. Toss to coat and serve.

Serving (1 cup) provides: 1 Fat, 4 Vegetables.

Per serving: 110 Calories, 5 g Total Fat, 1 g Saturated Fat, 0 mg Cholesterol, 151 mg Sodium, 16 g Total Carbohydrate, 3 g Dietary Fiber, 3 g Protein, 64 mg Calcium.

6

SALADS AND SIDE DISHES

Grilled Five-Vegetable Salad • Radish-Orange Salad

Grilled Corn–Red Pepper Salad • Grilled Panzanella • Middle Eastern
Grilled Eggplant–Lentil Salad

Pasta Salad with Grilled Vegetables • Brown Rice Salad with Vegetables

Barley Salad with Grilled Leeks and Mushrooms • Spicy Barbecued Beef Salad
with Grilled Potatoes and Onions

Asian Shrimp and Rice Salad • Grilled Tuna Niçoise Salad

Kansas City Barbecued Beans • Wild Rice–Grilled Mushroom Casserole

Charred Sweet Potatoes • Barbecued Sweet Potatoes • Orange–Grilled Potato Duo

Grilled Potato Wedges • Roasted Garlic Mashed Potatoes

Grilled Potato Salad • Grilled Polenta

GRILLED FIVE-VEGETABLE SALAD

This salad also makes a terrific sandwich filling. Grill the vegetables ahead and they will keep, tightly wrapped, in the refrigerator for several days. Using a grill basket ensures you won't lose any veggies to the coals.

Makes 4 servings

2 tablespoons fresh lemon juice
2 tablespoons balsamic vinegar
1 teaspoon Dijon-style mustard
1 garlic clove, minced
1/2 teaspoon salt
1/4 teaspoon freshly ground black pepper
1 tablespoon + 1 teaspoon olive oil

2 medium leeks, trimmed, well-washed and cut into 1/4" slices
2 medium zucchini, cut into 1/4" slices
2 heads Belgian endive, trimmed and cut into 1/4" slices
2 medium heads radicchio, trimmed and cut into 1/4" slices
24 asparagus spears, trimmed

1. Prepare grill for a medium fire, using direct method (see page xiii). Spray grill basket with nonstick cooking spray.
2. In small bowl, combine juice, vinegar, mustard, garlic, salt and pepper; whisk in oil a little at a time. Set aside.
3. Arrange leeks in a single layer in prepared basket; grill, covered, over medium heat, 5 minutes per side. Remove cover and grill another 2 minutes per side. Transfer to serving bowl.
4. Repeat grilling procedure with zucchini, endive, radicchio and asparagus, grilling each 3 minutes per side covered, and 1 minute per side uncovered.
5. Drizzle dressing over vegetables and toss gently to coat. Divide evenly among 4 plates and serve warm or chilled.

Serving (1 generous cup) provides: 1 Fat, 3 1/2 Vegetables.

Per serving: 104 Calories, 5 g Total Fat, 1 g Saturated Fat, 0 mg Cholesterol, 307 mg Sodium, 13 g Total Carbohydrate, 3 g Dietary Fiber, 5 g Protein, 71 mg Calcium.

RADISH-ORANGE SALAD

Crisp, tangy and refreshing, this salad is a perfect foil for spicy barbecue—and it won't weigh you down the way coleslaw can.

Makes 6 servings

3 small oranges
1/4 cup fresh lime juice
1 tablespoon peanut oil
1/2 teaspoon ground coriander

Freshly ground black pepper, to taste
1 1/2 cups thinly sliced radishes
6 medium celery stalks, thinly sliced

1. With paring knife, cut off the peel, including the white pith, from each orange. Cut peeled orange horizontally into 1" slices. Stack slices and cut into quarters.
2. In small bowl, whisk together juice, oil, coriander and pepper.
3. Place the orange pieces, radishes and celery in medium serving bowl. Drizzle dressing over oranges and vegetables and toss gently to coat. Divide evenly among 6 plates and serve.

Serving (1 cup) provides: 1/2 Fat, 1/2 Fruit, 1 Vegetable.

Per serving: 61 Calories, 3 g Total Fat, 0 g Saturated Fat, 0 mg Cholesterol, 33 mg Sodium, 10 g Total Carbohydrate, 3 g Dietary Fiber, 1 g Protein, 46 mg Calcium.

GRILLED CORN—RED PEPPER SALAD

This salad is versatile enough to accompany an elegant dinner or go along on a tailgate picnic.

Makes 4 servings

1 tablespoon snipped fresh dill
1 tablespoon fresh lemon juice
1 tablespoon Dijon-style mustard
$^1/_2$ teaspoon salt
$^1/_2$ teaspoon freshly ground
   black pepper
$^1/_2$ garlic clove, minced
$^1/_4$ cup carrot juice
1 tablespoon + 1 teaspoon olive oil

2 cups grilled corn kernels (see
   page 162)
$^1/_2$ cup chopped roasted red pepper
   (page 161)
$^1/_2$ cup diced celery
$^1/_2$ cup diced jicama*
$^1/_4$ cup chopped scallions
$^1/_4$ cup minced fresh parsley

1. In food processor, combine dill, lemon juice, mustard, salt, black pepper and garlic; purée until smooth. Add carrot juice and, while machine is running, slowly add oil; set aside.
2. In medium bowl, combine corn, red pepper, celery, jicama, scallions and parsley. Drizzle dressing over vegetables and toss gently to coat. Divide evenly among 4 plates and serve.

Serving (1 cup) provides: 1 Fat, 1 Vegetable, 1 Bread.

Per serving: 159 Calories, 6 g Total Fat, 1 g Saturated Fat, 0 mg Cholesterol, 436 mg Sodium, 27 g Total Carbohydrate, 4 g Dietary Fiber, 3 g Protein, 32 mg Calcium.

---

*Jicama (pronounced HEE-kah-mah), a large bulbous root vegetable with a sweet nutty taste, is available in Latino grocery stores and some supermarkets.

GRILLED PANZANELLA

Panzanella, an Italian bread salad, is a terrific way to use up day-old bread. Pour the dressing over the salad a few minutes before serving so that the bread can soak up the flavors.

Makes 4 servings

4 ounces day-old French or Italian bread, cut into $1/2$" slices
2 medium tomatoes, cubed
$1/2$ cup sliced cucumber rounds, halved
$1/2$ cup chopped scallions
2 tablespoons rinsed drained capers

2 tablespoons minced fresh basil
2 tablespoons red wine vinegar
1 tablespoon + 1 teaspoon olive oil
1 garlic clove, minced
$1/4$ teaspoon salt
$1/4$ teaspoon freshly ground black pepper

1. Prepare grill for a hot fire, using direct method (see page xiii).
2. Grill bread about 3 minutes, turning once, until crisp and browned on both sides. Cut into $1/2$" cubes.
3. In large shallow bowl, combine grilled bread, tomatoes, cucumber, scallions, capers and basil.
4. In small bowl, whisk together vinegar, oil, garlic, salt and pepper. Drizzle dressing over bread mixture and toss gently to coat. Let stand 5 minutes; divide evenly among 4 plates and serve.

Serving (1 cup) provides: 1 Fat, $1^1/2$ Vegetables, 1 Bread.

Per serving: 143 Calories, 6 g Total Fat, 1 g Saturated Fat, 0 mg Cholesterol, 427 mg Sodium, 20 g Total Carbohydrate, 2 g Dietary Fiber, 4 g Protein, 51 mg Calcium.

MIDDLE EASTERN GRILLED EGGPLANT– LENTIL SALAD

A variety of flavors and textures makes this salad special. The lentils and strips of grilled eggplant, lightly seasoned with cumin and garlic, contrast nicely with the refreshing crunch of cucumber. This is a perfect salad to take on a picnic.

Makes 4 servings

$1/4$ cup + 1 tablespoon fresh
   lemon juice
2 teaspoons olive oil
1 garlic clove, minced
$3/4$ teaspoon ground cumin
$1/4$ teaspoon salt
$1/4$ teaspoon freshly ground
   black pepper
$3/4$ cup vegetable broth

3 garlic cloves, peeled
$4 1/2$ ounces lentils, rinsed and
   drained
2 small onions, unpeeled
1 medium eggplant, pared and cut
   lengthwise into $1/2$" slices
6 cherry tomatoes, quartered
1 cup diced pared cucumber
2 teaspoons vegetable oil

1. Prepare grill for a medium fire, using direct method (see page xiii).
2. In small bowl, whisk together 3 tablespoons of the juice, the olive oil, minced garlic, $1/4$ teaspoon of the cumin, the salt and $1/8$ teaspoon of the pepper; set aside.
3. In small saucepan, combine broth, peeled garlic and another $1/4$ teaspoon of the cumin. Bring to a boil; add lentils. Simmer, covered, stirring occasionally, until lentils are tender but still firm, about 30 minutes. Remove from heat and set aside to cool. Remove garlic cloves and reserve.
4. In another small saucepan, cook onions in enough boiling water to cover until a sharp knife can just pierce center, 8–10 minutes. Remove from heat; drain and let cool. Remove skins and halve onions lengthwise; thread onto 12" metal skewer.
5. Brush both sides of eggplant slices and skewered onions with juice mixture; grill, turning occasionally and brushing with mixture until vegetables are tender, about 15 minutes for eggplant and 10 minutes for onions. Let cool.
6. Dice onions and cut eggplant into 1" strips. Transfer to medium bowl; stir in lentils, tomatoes and cucumber.

7. In small bowl, mash reserved garlic cloves with fork. Whisk in remaining 2 tablespoons of the juice, the vegetable oil, the remaining $^1/_4$ teaspoon of the cumin and the remaining $^1/_8$ teaspoon of the pepper. Drizzle dressing over lentil mixture and toss gently to coat. Serve at once, or cover and refrigerate; bring to room temperature. Divide evenly among 4 plates and serve.

Serving (about 1 $^1/_2$ cups) provides: 1 Fat, 3 Vegetables, 1 $^1/_2$ Proteins, 4 Optional Calories.

Per serving: 211 Calories, 5 g Total Fat, 1 g Saturated Fat, 0 mg Cholesterol, 335 mg Sodium, 33 g Total Carbohydrate, 6 g Dietary Fiber, 11 g Protein, 76 mg Calcium.

PASTA SALAD WITH GRILLED VEGETABLES

Grilled vegetables add so much flavor to this salad that you don't need a heavy dressing.

Makes 8 servings

12 ounces ziti or penne pasta

1 medium zucchini, cut lengthwise into $1/2$" slices

$1/2$ small eggplant, cut lengthwise into $1/2$" slices

1 medium red bell pepper, quartered

2 medium carrots, cut lengthwise into $1/4$" slices

$1/2$ cup finely chopped onion

$1/4$ cup orange juice

2 tablespoons olive oil

1 tablespoon plain nonfat yogurt

1 teaspoon Dijon-style mustard

$1/4$ teaspoon salt

Freshly ground black pepper, to taste

1. Prepare grill for a hot fire, using direct method (see page xiii).
2. Meanwhile, in large pot of boiling water, cook pasta 12–14 minutes, until tender. Drain and place in serving bowl; set aside and keep warm.
3. Grill zucchini, eggplant, bell pepper and carrots about 8–10 minutes, turning once, until slightly charred and fork-tender. Let cool; cut into bite-size pieces. Add with onion to pasta.
4. In small bowl, whisk together juice, oil, yogurt, mustard, salt and black pepper. Drizzle dressing over salad and toss well to coat. Divide evenly among 8 plates and serve immediately.

Serving (1 cup) provides: $3/4$ Fat, 1 Vegetable, 2 Breads, 5 Optional Calories.

Per serving: 219 Calories, 4 g Total Fat, 1 g Saturated Fat, 0 mg Cholesterol, 98 mg Sodium, 39 g Total Carbohydrate, 3 g Dietary Fiber, 7 g Protein, 33 mg Calcium.

BROWN RICE SALAD WITH VEGETABLES

This delicious nutty salad can be made a day ahead and stored, covered, in the refrigerator. Slice the vegetables on the diagonal for a pretty effect.

Makes 4 servings

8 ounces short-grain brown rice
1 medium carrot, cut into
  1/4" slices
1/2 cup chopped scallions
1/2 medium zucchini, cut into
  1/4" slices
1/2 cup low-sodium
  chicken broth
2 tablespoons fresh lemon juice

1 tablespoon + 1 teaspoon olive oil
1 teaspoon minced fresh
  thyme leaves
1/2 teaspoon salt
1/4 teaspoon freshly ground
  black pepper
3/4 cup dried currants
2 tablespoons minced fresh parsley

1. In medium saucepan, combine rice with two cups water; cover and bring to a boil over medium-high heat. Reduce heat to medium-low; simmer 40–45 minutes. Remove from heat; uncover and let cool.
2. Prepare grill for a medium fire, using direct method (see page xiii). Spray grill basket with nonstick cooking spray.
3. Meanwhile, in small saucepan over medium-high heat, bring 1/4 cup water to a boil; add carrots, cook 3 minutes and drain.
4. Layer carrots, scallions and zucchini in prepared grill basket; grill 6 minutes, turning once; transfer vegetables to plate.
5. In small bowl, whisk together broth, juice, oil, thyme, salt and pepper; stir into brown rice. Add currants and toss to combine.
6. Spoon rice mixture into serving bowl and surround with grilled carrots, scallions and zucchini, overlapping pieces and alternating colors; sprinkle with parsley. Divide evenly among 4 plates and serve.

Serving (1 cup) provides: 1 Fat, 1 1/2 Fruits, 1 Vegetable, 2 Breads, 3 Optional Calories.

Per serving: 350 Calories, 7 g Total Fat, 1 g Saturated Fat, 0 mg Cholesterol, 308 mg Sodium, 69 g Total Carbohydrate, 5 g Dietary Fiber, 7 g Protein, 64 mg Calcium.

BARLEY SALAD WITH GRILLED LEEKS AND MUSHROOMS

This delicately flavored salad makes an excellent accompaniment to grilled meat, fish or poultry. When served with a loaf of crusty bread, it makes a superb vegetarian main course, perfect for lunch or a light dinner.

Makes 4 servings

2 garlic cloves
³/₄ cup reduced-sodium
   vegetable broth
1 bay leaf
³/₈ teaspoon dried thyme leaves,
   crumbled
4 ¹/₂ ounces barley
3 medium leeks (1 ¹/₂ pounds),
   well-washed

6 ounces medium mushrooms,
   trimmed
1 tablespoon + 1 teaspoon
   vegetable oil
1 tablespoon + 1 teaspoon
   red wine vinegar
¹/₈ teaspoon salt
¹/₈ teaspoon freshly ground
   black pepper

1. Halve one garlic clove and mince the other; set aside.
2. In medium saucepan, combine 1 cup water, the broth, bay leaf, ¹/₈ teaspoon of the thyme and the garlic halves; bring to a boil. Add barley; reduce heat to low and simmer, covered, until tender, 35–40 minutes. Remove from heat; transfer to medium bowl, discarding bay leaf and reserving garlic halves.
3. Preheat grill for a medium fire, using direct method (see page xiii). Spray grill rack evenly with nonstick cooking spray (see page xv). If using wooden skewers, soak in water 30 minutes.
4. Remove root ends and all but 3" of green tops from leeks; cut into 1" slices. Put leeks in medium saucepan with enough water to cover. Bring to a boil, reduce heat to low and simmer until leeks are barely tender, about 10 minutes. Drain and let cool. Cut leeks and mushrooms in half lengthwise; thread leeks onto three 12" metal or wooden skewers, and mushrooms onto 3 more skewers.
5. In small bowl, mash reserved garlic with fork. Add oil, 2 teaspoons of the vinegar, the salt, pepper and remaining ¹/₄ teaspoon of the thyme; whisk together. Reserve 1 tablespoon of basting sauce in small bowl for dressing.

6. Brush leeks and mushrooms with basting sauce. Place on prepared rack and grill, turning and brushing occasionally, until vegetables are tender, 5–7 minutes for mushrooms and 10–12 minutes for leeks. Let cool. Remove vegetables from skewers; chop into $1/2$" pieces. Add to barley.

7. Whisk remaining 2 teaspoons vinegar and the minced garlic into reserved dressing. Drizzle dressing over barley mixture and toss gently to coat. Divide evenly among 4 plates and serve.

Serving (about 1 cup) provides: 1 Fat, 1 Vegetable, 1 $1/2$ Breads, 3 Optional Calories.

Per serving: 217 Calories, 6 g Total Fat, 1 g Saturated Fat, 0 mg Cholesterol, 137 mg Sodium, 37 g Total Carbohydrate, 7 g Dietary Fiber, 6 g Protein, 65 mg Calcium.

SPICY BARBECUED BEEF SALAD WITH GRILLED POTATOES AND ONIONS

This spicy main-dish salad is for meat-and-potato lovers. Double the amount of marinade and flank steak and serve half the steak hot one day, then slice the rest for this salad the following day.

Makes 4 servings

1 cup tomato juice
2 tablespoons red wine vinegar
1 tablespoon chili powder
1 tablespoon Worcestershire sauce
$^1/_2$ teaspoon garlic powder
$^1/_4$ teaspoon ground red pepper
    or hot red pepper sauce

5 ounces trimmed flank steak,
    pierced on both sides with fork
Ten 2-ounce new potatoes,
    scrubbed
2 medium onions, unpeeled
12 cherry tomatoes, halved
2 teaspoons vegetable oil

1. Prepare grill for a medium fire, using direct method (see page xiii). If using wooden skewers, soak in water 30 minutes.
2. Combine $^3/_4$ cup of the tomato juice, the vinegar, chili powder, Worcestershire sauce, garlic powder and red pepper; reserve 3 tablespoons of mixture in small bowl for dressing. Add steak and marinate 1 hour, turning after 30 minutes (see page xvi). (If you prefer milder barbecue flavor, marinate 40 minutes, turning after 20 minutes.)
3. Place potatoes, onions and cold water to cover in medium saucepan; bring to a boil, reduce heat and simmer until potatoes are barely tender, 8–10 minutes. Drain and let cool. Peel and halve onions; halve potatoes. Thread 5 potato halves onto each of four 12" metal or wooden skewers and 2 onion halves onto 2 more skewers.
4. Remove steak from marinade. Drain marinade into small saucepan. Bring to a rolling boil; boil for one minute, stirring constantly. Remove from heat.
5. Grill steak, turning once, 12 minutes (medium) or 15 minutes (well-done). Brush potatoes and onions with marinade. Grill vegetables, turning and brushing occasionally, until tender and lightly browned, 8–10 minutes.
6. Remove from heat; let steak stand 5 minutes before slicing across grain into thin diagonal slices. Chop cooked potatoes and onions into $^3/_4$" chunks. Place steak, potatoes and onions in medium bowl; add tomatoes.

7. Whisk remaining ¹/₄ cup tomato juice and the oil into reserved marinade. Drizzle dressing over salad and toss gently to coat. Cover and refrigerate at least 1 hour to blend flavors. Divide evenly among 4 plates and serve.

Serving (about 1 ²/₃ cups) provides: ¹/₂ Fat, 2 Vegetables, 1 Protein, 1 Bread.

Per serving: 238 Calories, 6 g Total Fat, 2 g Saturated Fat, 19 mg Cholesterol, 319 mg Sodium, 35 g Total Carbohydrate, 4 g Dietary Fiber, 12 g Protein, 23 mg Calcium.

ASIAN SHRIMP AND RICE SALAD

Makes 4 servings

$^1/_3$ cup + 2 tablespoons pineapple
juice
2 tablespoons reduced-sodium
soy sauce
1 fluid ounce (2 tablespoons)
dry sherry
1 medium garlic clove, minced
$^1/_2$ teaspoon ground ginger
8 ounces medium shrimp,
peeled and deveined

2 teaspoons Chinese sesame oil*
$^1/_2$ teaspoon fresh lemon juice
2 cups cooled cooked white rice
$^3/_4$ cup snow peas, cut into
$^1/_2$" lengths
$^1/_2$ cup diced pared fresh pineapple
(or drained canned unsweetened
chunks)
$^1/_4$ cup sliced scallions

1. Prepare grill for a medium fire, using direct method (see page xiii). If using wooden skewers, soak in water 30 minutes.
2. Combine 1/3 cup of the pineapple juice, the soy sauce, sherry, half of the garlic and $^1/_4$ teaspoon of the ginger; reserve 2 tablespoons of mixture in medium bowl for dressing. Add shrimp to remaining mixture and marinate 30 minutes (see page xvi). Remove shrimp; discard marinade.
3. Thread 4 shrimp onto each of four 12" metal or wooden skewers; grill, turning occasionally, until shrimp are opaque, 3–5 minutes. Let cool. Remove shrimp from skewers; halve each lengthwise and set aside.
4. To prepare dressing, whisk the remaining 2 tablespoons pineapple juice, the oil, lemon juice, and the remaining garlic and $^1/_4$ teaspoon ginger into reserved marinade.
5. In another medium bowl, combine rice, snow peas, pineapple, scallions and reserved shrimp; drizzle dressing over salad and toss to coat. Cover with plastic wrap and refrigerate at least 1 hour. Divide evenly among 4 plates and serve.

Serving (about 1 $^1/_4$ cups) provides: $^1/_2$ Fat, $^1/_2$ Fruit, $^1/_2$ Vegetable, 1 Protein, 1 Bread, 10 Optional Calories.

Per serving: 266 Calories, 4 g Total Fat, 1 g Saturated Fat, 86 mg Cholesterol, 389 mg Sodium, 39 g Total Carbohydrate, 1 g Dietary Fiber, 16 g Protein, 64 mg Calcium.

*Available in most grocery stores, Chinese sesame oil adds an intense sesame flavor integral to this salad. If you substitute regular sesame oil or vegetable oil, the flavor will be very different.

GRILLED TUNA NIÇOISE SALAD

Makes 4 servings

2 tablespoons fresh lemon juice
1 tablespoon white wine vinegar
2 teaspoons Dijon-style mustard
1 tablespoon olive oil
Two 10-ounce tuna steaks
1/2 teaspoon salt
1/4 teaspoon freshly ground
  black pepper
1 pound 4 ounces small new
  potatoes, scrubbed and halved

1 cup green beans, washed
  and trimmed
6 cups romaine lettuce, washed and
  torn into bite-size pieces
2 medium tomatoes, cut into
  eighths
4 anchovy fillets, rinsed and drained
10 small pitted black olives, halved
1/4 cup minced fresh basil

1. Prepare grill for a medium-hot fire, using direct method (see page xiii).
2. To prepare dressing, in small bowl, combine juice, vinegar and mustard; whisk in oil a little at a time. Set aside.
3. Season tuna with salt and pepper; grill 3–5 minutes per side, until cooked through. Cool to room temperature; cut into 1/4" slices or break into chunks.
4. Place potatoes in medium saucepan and cover with 2" cold water. Bring to a boil over high heat; reduce heat to medium and simmer 20 minutes, until tender. With slotted spoon, transfer potatoes to bowl of cold water; drain when completely cooled.
5. In medium saucepan, bring 2" water to a boil. Arrange green beans on steamer rack; place in saucepan and steam 4–6 minutes until tender-crisp. Rinse in colander under cold running water until completely cooled.
6. On large serving platter, arrange lettuce in low mound. Place potatoes, cut-side up, around the edge of lettuce; put string beans along the inside edge of potatoes. Place tomatoes along inside edge of string beans, and mound tuna in center. Lay anchovy fillets over tuna in crisscross pattern and spread olives around rim. Sprinkle basil over entire salad and drizzle with dressing. Divide evenly among 4 plates and serve.

Serving (about 2 1/2 cups) provides: 1 Fat, 4 1/2 Vegetables, 2 Proteins, 1 Bread, 8 Optional Calories.

Per serving: 422 Calories, 12 g Total Fat, 2 g Saturated Fat, 56 mg Cholesterol, 628 mg Sodium, 37 g Total Carbohydrate, 6 g Dietary Fiber, 40 g Protein, 100 mg Calcium.

KANSAS CITY BARBECUED BEANS

This terrific side dish stands up to the spiciest barbecue. Try it without turkey ham as a meatless main dish, with corn bread and your favorite grilled vegetables on the side.

Makes 6 servings

13 ¹/₂ ounces navy beans,
    picked over, rinsed and drained
1 tablespoon vegetable oil
1 ¹/₂ medium green bell peppers,
    seeded and diced
1 medium onion, finely chopped
3 ounces lean turkey ham, diced
    (optional)
1 cup tomato purée

¹/₂ cup apple cider
2 tablespoons dry mustard
2 tablespoons dark molasses
1 tablespoon Worcestershire
    sauce
1 tablespoon cider vinegar
1 teaspoon chili powder
2 tablespoons firmly packed dark
    brown sugar

1. Place beans in large saucepan and cover with 2" cold water. Cover and bring to boil over medium-high heat; reduce heat to low and simmer 2 minutes. Remove from heat and let stand, covered, 1 hour; drain in colander. Return beans to saucepan and repeat procedure, this time simmering beans until they are soft but still hold their shape, about 1 hour; drain.
2. Preheat oven to 350° F; spray 2-quart casserole with nonstick cooking spray.
3. Place large skillet over medium-high heat; heat oil 30 seconds more. Add peppers and onion and cook, stirring frequently, until onion is translucent, 5 minutes. Add turkey ham (if using) and cook 2 minutes more. Stir in tomato purée, cider, mustard, molasses, Worcestershire sauce, vinegar and chili powder; cover and cook until bubbling, about 3 minutes. Add beans and stir gently to coat.

4. Transfer bean mixture to prepared casserole; sprinkle evenly with brown sugar and cover with foil. Bake until beans have absorbed most of the sauce, 45 minutes; remove foil and bake 15 minutes more. Divide evenly among 6 plates and serve.

Serving (about $^3/_4$ cup, prepared without turkey ham) provides: $^1/_2$ Fat, 1 $^1/_2$ Vegetables, 2 Breads, 40 Optional Calories. With turkey ham: add 1 $^1/_2$ Proteins.

Per serving (without turkey ham): 234 Calories, 4 g Total Fat, 0 g Saturated Fat, 0 mg Cholesterol, 169 mg Sodium, 41 g Total Carbohydrate, 5 g Dietary Fiber, 11 g Protein, 143 mg Calcium.

Per serving (with turkey ham): 252 Calories, 4 g Total Fat, 1 g Saturated Fat, 9 mg Cholesterol, 310 mg Sodium, 42 g Total Carbohydrate, 5 g Dietary Fiber, 14 g Protein, 144 mg Calcium.

WILD RICE–GRILLED MUSHROOM CASSEROLE

Use either large mushrooms or portobello mushrooms. This dish can be baked ahead and reheated at serving time.

Makes 6 servings

4–5 large (2") mushrooms or
2–3 portobello mushrooms
(4 ounces), stemmed
1 tablespoon olive oil
$^1/_2$ cup minced shallots
2$^3/_4$ cups reduced-sodium
chicken or beef broth

6 ounces wild rice
$^1/_2$ teaspoon dried thyme or
rosemary leaves, crumbled
$^1/_2$ teaspoon freshly ground
black pepper
1 bay leaf

1. Prepare grill for a medium fire, using direct method (see page xiii).
2. Grill mushrooms at edge of fire, turning often, until lightly browned (not charred), about 5–10 minutes. Transfer to plate; dice and set aside.
3. Preheat oven to 350° F. Place medium saucepan over medium heat 30 seconds; heat oil 30 seconds more. Add shallots; cook, stirring frequently, until softened, about 4 minutes. Add broth, reserved mushrooms with any juices, the rice, thyme, pepper and bay leaf. Transfer to a 1-quart casserole. Cover and bake 1 hour, until liquid is absorbed and rice is tender but still slightly chewy. Divide evenly among 6 plates and serve.

Serving ($^1/_2$ cup) provides: $^1/_2$ Fat, $^1/_2$ Vegetable, 1 Bread, 9 Optional Calories.

Per serving: 145 Calories, 3 g Total Fat, 0 g Saturated Fat, 0 mg Cholesterol, 261 mg Sodium, 25 g Total Carbohydrate, 2 g Dietary Fiber, 6 g Protein, 16 mg Calcium.

CHARRED SWEET POTATOES

This is a simple recipe, and utterly delicious. Use the lighter-skinned variety of potato rather than the orange-red type (often labeled "yam"). Try this with Capon with Chocolate-Chipotle Sauce (page 36) or any pork dish.

Makes 4 servings

Four 6-ounce sweet potatoes, well-scrubbed

Lime wedges, for garnish

Minced fresh cilantro, for garnish (optional)

1. Prepare grill for a medium fire, using direct method (see page xiii); do not use grill rack.
2. When coals are covered with white ash, bury potatoes in coals and roast about 45 minutes, turning once, until potatoes can be pierced easily with barbecue fork.
3. Transfer potatoes to each of 4 plates. Cut potatoes in half and scoop out pulp, discarding skins. Serve with a squeeze of lime juice and sprinkle with cilantro (if using).

Serving (4 ¹/₂ ounces sweet potatoes) provides: 1 ¹/₂ Breads.

Per serving: 129 Calories, 0 g Total Fat, 0 g Saturated Fat, 0 mg Cholesterol, 16 mg Sodium, 30 g Total Carbohydrate, 4 g Dietary Fiber, 2 g Protein, 27 mg Calcium.

ORANGE–GRILLED POTATO DUO

Grilling potatoes adds wonderful depth to their inherently delicious texture and flavor. This simple maple glaze, with hints of orange, ginger and coriander, complements both sweet and new potatoes alike, adding sweetness and pungency. It's delicious on acorn or butternut squash as well.

Makes 4 servings

10 ounces new potatoes, scrubbed

8 ounces pared sweet potatoes, cut into sixteen 1" cubes

$^1/_3$ cup + 2 teaspoons fresh lemon juice

$^3/_4$ teaspoon grated orange zest*

$^1/_4$ cup fresh orange juice

2 teaspoons cornstarch

$^1/_4$ cup maple-flavored pancake syrup

2 teaspoons vegetable oil

1 $^1/_2$ teaspoons ground coriander

$^3/_4$ teaspoon ground ginger

$^1/_4$ teaspoon salt

$^1/_8$ teaspoon freshly ground black pepper

2 small oranges, peeled and sectioned, for garnish

1. Prepare grill for a medium fire, using direct method (see page xiii). Spray grill rack with nonstick cooking spray (see page xv). If using wooden skewers, soak in water 30 minutes.
2. Place new and sweet potatoes and cold water to cover in medium saucepan; bring to a boil, reduce heat and simmer uncovered, just until tender, about 10 minutes. Drain and let cool.
3. In small saucepan over medium-high heat, combine lemon juice, orange zest and juice and cornstarch. Stir in syrup, oil, coriander, ginger, salt and pepper. Cook, stirring constantly, until thickened; let cool.
4. Cut new potatoes into quarters; thread 5 pieces on each of four 12" metal or wooden skewers. Thread 4 sweet potato pieces on each of 4 more 12" skewers.

5. Place potatoes on prepared rack and brush with glaze (it will be thick; stir before using). Grill potatoes, turning occasionally and brushing with remaining glaze, until they are lightly browned and evenly glazed, 8–10 minutes.
6. Place 1 skewer each of new and sweet potatoes on each of 4 plates; garnish with orange sections and serve.

Serving (2 skewers) provides: $^1/_2$ Fat, $^1/_2$ Fruit, 1 Bread, 55 Optional Calories.

Per serving: 212 Calories, 3 g Total Fat, 0 g Saturated Fat, 0 mg Cholesterol, 169 mg Sodium, 46 g Total Carbohydrate, 3 g Dietary Fiber, 3 g Protein, 22 mg Calcium.

*The zest of the orange is the peel without any of the pith (white membrane). To remove zest from orange, use a zester or vegetable peeler. To grate zest, use a zester or the fine side of a vegetable grater.

BARBECUED SWEET POTATOES

Serve these spicy-sweet treats with burgers or grilled chicken.

Makes 4 servings

2 tablespoons + 2 teaspoons
ketchup
1 tablespoon Worcestershire sauce
1 tablespoon red wine vinegar
1 teaspoon yellow mustard

$1/2$ teaspoon freshly ground
black pepper
1 pound sweet potatoes, pared
and cut into $1/4$" slices

1. Prepare grill for a medium fire, using direct method (see page xiii).
2. In small bowl, combine ketchup, Worcestershire sauce, vinegar, mustard and pepper; mix well.
3. Brush potato slices on both sides with ketchup mixture. Grill, turning frequently and brushing with remaining ketchup mixture, 4 minutes per side.
4. Divide evenly among 4 plates and serve immediately.

Serving (3 ounces sweet potatoes) provides: 1 Bread, 10 Optional Calories.

Per serving: 104 Calories, 0 g Total Fat, 0 g Saturated Fat, 0 mg Cholesterol, 188 mg Sodium, 24 g Total Carbohydrate, 3 g Dietary Fiber, 2 g Protein, 25 mg Calcium.

GRILLED POTATO WEDGES

Serve these plain, or top them with a sprinkle of vinegar, a dollop of low-fat yogurt or sour cream, a grating of sharp cheddar cheese or the juices from grilled meat or poultry.

Makes 4 servings

1 tablespoon + 1 teaspoon olive oil
$^1/_4$ teaspoon ground red
   pepper, or to taste
$^1/_4$ teaspoon onion powder

$^1/_4$ teaspoon liquid smoke
Four 5-ounce baking potatoes,
   well-scrubbed and quartered
   lengthwise

1. Prepare grill for a medium fire, using direct method (see page xiii).
2. In medium bowl, combine oil, pepper, onion powder and liquid smoke; add potatoes and toss to coat.
3. Place potato wedges along edges of grill. Turn every 7 minutes and move wedges closer to the center with each turn. Grill about 20 minutes or until tender when pierced with barbecue fork or sharp knife. Divide evenly among 4 plates and serve immediately.

Serving (4 wedges) provides: 1 Fat, 1 Bread.

Per serving: 212 Calories, 5 g Total Fat, 1 g Saturated Fat, 38 mg Cholesterol, 16 mg Sodium, 38 g Total Carbohydrate, 4 g Dietary Fiber, 4 g Protein, 1 mg Calcium.

ROASTED GARLIC MASHED POTATOES

Roasted garlic has a buttery-sweet flavor that turns mashed potatoes into a "wicked good" yet healthful delight. Roasting also tames garlic's pungency, so don't be alarmed at the quantity in this recipe.

Makes 8 servings

2 pounds 8 ounces baking
    potatoes, pared and cut into
    1" cubes
2 heads Roasted Garlic (page 159)
$^1/_2$ cup hot skim milk

$^1/_2$ cup hot evaporated skimmed
    milk
$^1/_2$ teaspoon salt
$^1/_4$ teaspoon freshly ground
    black pepper

1. Place potatoes and cold water to cover in large saucepan; bring to a boil; reduce heat and simmer, uncovered, just until tender, about 10–15 minutes. Drain, reserving liquid. Return potatoes to saucepan and shake over low heat until they appear floury, about 2–3 minutes; remove from heat.
2. Slice tops off roasted garlic heads and squeeze pulp out of each clove into a large bowl.
3. Force potatoes and roasted garlic through ricer or food mill into medium bowl. Whisk in milk, evaporated milk, salt and pepper; thin to desired consistency with reserved potato water. Divide evenly among 8 plates and serve at once.

Serving (1 cup) provides: $^1/_4$ Vegetable, 1 Bread, 15 Optional Calories.

Per serving: 127 Calories, 0 g Total Fat, 0 g Saturated Fat, 1 mg Cholesterol, 174 mg Sodium, 27 g Total Carbohydrate, 2 g Dietary Fiber, 5 g Protein, 93 mg Calcium.

GRILLED POTATO SALAD

Serve this creamy potato salad alongside burgers or barbecued chicken.

Makes 4 servings

1 pound 4 ounces new potatoes,
  cut into 1" slices
2 tablespoons white wine vinegar
2 tablespoons fresh lemon juice
1 garlic clove, minced
$^1/_2$ teaspoon salt
$^1/_4$ teaspoon paprika

$^1/_8$ teaspoon ground red pepper
$^3/_4$ cup yogurt cheese*
$^1/_2$ cup chopped scallions
$^1/_4$ cup minced fresh parsley
2 medium Spanish onions,
  separated into rings

1. Prepare grill for a medium-hot fire, using direct method (see page xiii); spray grill basket with nonstick cooking spray.
2. Place potatoes and cold water to cover in medium saucepan; bring to a boil, reduce heat and simmer 20 minutes, until potatoes are tender. Drain and set aside.
3. In mini food processor, combine vinegar, juice, garlic, salt, paprika and pepper. Pulse several times to mix. Add yogurt cheese and purée just until smooth. Transfer to medium bowl; stir in scallions and parsley and set aside.
4. Grill cooked potatoes and the onion rings in prepared grill basket, turning frequently, 8–10 minutes, until onions are tender and potatoes are browned.
5. Coarsely chop grilled onions and add to dressing in bowl. Add potatoes and mix well. Divide evenly among 4 plates and serve.

Serving (1 cup) provides: $^1/_2$ Milk, $^3/_4$ Vegetable, 1 Bread.

Per serving: 170 Calories, 0 g Total Fat, 0 g Saturated Fat, 0 mg Cholesterol, 321 mg Sodium, 35 g Total Carbohydrate, 4 g Dietary Fiber, 7 g Protein, 131 mg Calcium.

*To prepare yogurt cheese, spoon 1 $^1/_2$ cups plain nonfat yogurt into coffee filter or cheesecloth-lined strainer; place over bowl. Refrigerate, covered, at least 5 hours or overnight. Discard liquid in bowl. Makes $^3/_4$ cup yogurt cheese.

GRILLED POLENTA

If you add cheese to this polenta, it becomes a delicious entrée—serve with some grilled vegetables or with Grilled Ratatouille (page 103).

Makes 4 servings

1 teaspoon salt (reduce to
¹/₂ teaspoon, if using cheese)
6 ounces coarse polenta*
or cornmeal
1 tablespoon + 1 teaspoon
olive oil

3 ounces Parmesan cheese, grated
(optional)
¹/₂ teaspoon freshly ground
black pepper

1. Spray an 8×4" loaf pan with nonstick cooking spray.
2. In lower half of double boiler, bring 2" water to a boil; reduce heat to low and simmer. In upper half of double boiler bring 2 cups water to a boil over high heat; add salt.
3. In medium bowl, combine 1 ¹/₂ cups water with the polenta and oil; pour into upper half of double boiler, stirring constantly. Place upper half of double boiler over lower half; cover and cook 20 minutes. Stir in cheese (if using) and pepper. Spread polenta evenly into prepared pan; smooth top. Cover and chill overnight.
4. Prepare grill for a medium fire, using direct method (see page xiii).
5. Invert loaf pan to release polenta. Slice polenta into eight 1" slices. Grill directly over hot coals about 3 minutes, until lightly crisp and brown; turn and grill 3–4 minutes longer. Divide evenly among 4 plates and serve.

Serving (2 slices, without cheese) provides: 1 Fat, 2 Breads. With cheese: add 1 Protein.

Per serving (without cheese and with 1 teaspoon salt): 198 Calories, 5 g Total Fat, 1 g Saturated Fat, 0 mg Cholesterol, 552 mg Sodium, 33 g Total Carbohydrate, 2 g Dietary Fiber, 4 g Protein, 7 mg Calcium.

Per serving (with cheese and ¹/₂ teaspoon salt): 281 Calories, 11 g Total Fat, 4 g Saturated Fat, 14 mg Cholesterol, 615 mg Sodium, 34 g Total Carbohydrate, 2 g Dietary Fiber, 11 g Protein, 257 mg Calcium.

Polenta is a type of cornmeal used throughout northern Italy to make cornmeal mush, also called polenta. It can be found in well-stocked supermarkets and gourmet grocery stores.

7

PIZZAS AND BREADS

Pizza Dough • Mozzarella, Tomato and Basil Pizza

Grilled Chicken–Artichoke Pizza • Shrimp Toast Pizza

Potato, Onion and Olive Pizza • Apple, Raisin, Feta Cheese & Carrot Pizza

Blue Cheese and Pear Pizza • Herbed Pita Bread

Skillet-Grilled Cornbread • Corn and Rice Spoonbread

PIZZA DOUGH

This recipe will yield two 8" crusts. If you're feeding a crowd, it can easily be doubled. Just use what you need, then divide remaining dough into pizza-size portions, wrap tightly in freezer wrap, and freeze. Thaw in the refrigerator 4 hours before using.

Makes 4 servings

1 ¼ teaspoons active dry yeast
(about half ¼-ounce packet)
½ cup lukewarm water
(105–115° F.)
⅛ teaspoon granulated sugar
2 tablespoons cornmeal

1 teaspoon olive oil
½ teaspoon salt
1 ¼ cups + 1 tablespoon
all-purpose flour (reserve
1 tablespoon)

1. In large bowl, sprinkle yeast over water, stir in sugar; let stand 3 minutes until foamy. Stir in cornmeal, oil and salt.
2. Using wooden spoon, gradually stir in flour until stiff dough forms and all flour is incorporated.
3. Sprinkle work surface with reserved flour. Turn dough out onto prepared work surface and knead 3 minutes, until dough is smooth and elastic.
4. Spray large bowl with nonstick cooking spray; place dough in bowl. Cover loosely with plastic wrap or damp towel and let rise in warm, draft-free place until dough doubles in volume, about 1 ½ hours.
5. Punch down dough; form into ball and let rise in covered bowl 30 minutes more. With knife, divide dough in half. Proceed with pizza recipe or wrap tightly in freezer wrap and freeze.

Serving (one-fourth of dough, or one-half the crust of an 8" pie) provides: ¼ Fat, 2 Breads.

Per serving: 181 Calories, 2 g Total Fat, 0 g Saturated Fat, 0 mg Cholesterol, 275 mg Sodium, 35 g Total Carbohydrate, 2 g Dietary Fiber, 5 g Protein, 9 mg Calcium.

MOZZARELLA, TOMATO AND BASIL PIZZA

This most basic pizza, known as Pizza Margherita in Italy, proves the old adage that less is more. Use the freshest basil and tomatoes you can find.

Makes 4 servings

1 tablespoon all-purpose flour
1 recipe Pizza Dough (page 132)
2 tablespoons finely chopped
   shallots
1 1/2 ounces skim-milk mozzarella
   cheese, finely shredded

2 small plum tomatoes, thinly
   sliced
1/4 cup whole fresh basil leaves,
   firmly packed

1. Prepare grill for a hot fire, using direct method (see page xiii).
2. Sprinkle work surface with flour. With rolling pin, roll out dough to two 8" circles, approximately 1/8" thick.
3. Carefully lift dough directly onto grill rack. Grill about 2 minutes, until dough bubbles and begins to char on bottom; turn. Sprinkle crusts evenly with shallots; evenly distribute one-fourth of the cheese over each. Arrange tomato slices and basil leaves evenly over cheese and top with remaining cheese. Close grill cover or tent with foil. Grill 3–5 minutes, until cheese is melted and crust is crisp. Cut into quarters and serve.

Serving (one-half of 8" pie) provides: 1/4 Fat, 1/4 Vegetable, 1/2 Protein, 2 Breads, 8 Optional Calories.

Per serving: 231 Calories, 4 g Total Fat, 1 g Saturated Fat, 6 mg Cholesterol, 328 mg Sodium, 40 g Total Carbohydrate, 2 g Dietary Fiber, 8 g Protein, 107 mg Calcium.

GRILLED CHICKEN—ARTICHOKE PIZZA

These pizzas are a snap to cook, and even a small amount of toppings gives them lots of flavor.

Makes 4 servings

1 tablespoon all-purpose flour
1 recipe Pizza Dough
   (see page 132)
2 tablespoons finely chopped
   shallots
³/₄ ounce Gruyère cheese,
   finely shredded

2 ounces grilled chicken, shredded
   (try Grill-Roasted Chicken with
   Garlic-Rosemary Rub, page 18)
1 ¹/₂ cups artichoke hearts, drained,
   rinsed and quartered
¹/₄ cup chopped scallions

1. Prepare grill for a hot fire, using direct method (see page xiii).
2. Sprinkle work surface with flour. With rolling pin, roll out dough to two 8" circles, approximately ¹/₈" thick.
3. Carefully lift dough directly onto grill rack. Grill about 2 minutes, until dough bubbles and begins to char on bottom; turn. Sprinkle crusts evenly with shallots; evenly distribute one-fourth of the cheese over each. Arrange chicken and artichokes evenly over cheese, sprinkle with scallions and top with remaining cheese. Close grill cover or tent with foil. Grill 3–5 minutes, until cheese is melted and crust is crisp. Cut into quarters and serve.

Serving (one-half of 8" pie) provides: ¹/₄ Fat, ³/₄ Vegetable, ³/₄ Protein, 2 Breads, 8 Optional Calories.

Per serving: 282 Calories, 5 g Total Fat, 2 g Saturated Fat, 19 mg Cholesterol, 430 mg Sodium, 46 g Total Carbohydrate, 3 g Dietary Fiber, 14 g Protein, 100 mg Calcium.

SHRIMP TOAST PIZZA

If you enjoy shrimp toast in Chinese restaurants, you'll love this clever pizza topping.

Makes 4 servings

10 ounces large or medium
   shrimp, peeled and deveined
$^1/_2$ cup chopped scallions
2 ounces water chestnuts
1 egg white
$^1/_2$ fluid ounce (1 tablespoon)
   dry sherry
2 teaspoons cornstarch

2 teaspoons grated pared fresh
   ginger root
2 teaspoons sesame oil
$^1/_4$ teaspoon salt
1 tablespoon all-purpose flour
1 recipe Pizza Dough (page 132)
Crushed red pepper flakes, to taste

1. Prepare grill for a hot fire, using direct method (see page xiii).
2. In food processor or blender, combine shrimp, scallions, water chestnuts, egg white, sherry, cornstarch, ginger, 1 teaspoon of the oil and the salt. Process to a slightly chunky paste.
3. Sprinkle work surface with flour. With rolling pin, roll out dough to two 8" circles, approximately $^1/_8$" thick.
4. Carefully lift dough directly onto grill rack. Brush $^1/_2$ teaspoon of remaining oil over top of each crust. Grill about 2 minutes, until dough bubbles and begins to char on bottom; turn. Spread half of the shrimp mixture evenly over cooked surface of each crust; sprinkle each with pepper flakes, to taste. Close grill cover or tent with foil. Grill 3–5 minutes, until topping is pink and crust is crisp. Cut into quarters and serve.

Serving (one-half of 8" pie) provides: $^3/_4$ Fat, $^1/_4$ Vegetable, 1 Protein, 2 Breads, 35 Optional Calories.

Per serving: 303 Calories, 5 g Total Fat, 1 g Saturated Fat, 86 mg Cholesterol, 512 mg Sodium, 43 g Total Carbohydrate, 2 g Dietary Fiber, 18 g Protein, 51 mg Calcium.

POTATO, ONION AND OLIVE PIZZA

You may never have thought of a pizza topping like this—but once you've tried it, you may just switch from the usual tomato-and-cheese!

Makes 4 servings

2 teaspoons olive oil
5 ounces thinly sliced red potato
2 cups thinly sliced onions
1 tablespoon all-purpose flour
1 recipe Pizza Dough (page 132)

6 large kalamata olives, pitted
   and chopped
$^1/_2$ cup chopped arugula
2 tablespoons freshly grated
   Parmesan cheese

1. Prepare grill for a hot fire, using direct method (see page xiii).
2. Place small nonstick skillet over medium heat 30 seconds. Heat $^1/_2$ teaspoon of the oil 30 seconds. Add potatoes; cook, stirring constantly, until browned and soft, 15–18 minutes. Transfer to plate.
3. Return skillet to heat; heat another $^1/_2$ teaspoon of the oil 30 seconds. Add onions; cook, stirring constantly, until soft and golden, about 5 minutes. Remove from heat.
4. Sprinkle work surface with flour. With rolling pin, roll out dough to two 8" circles, approximately $^1/_8$" thick.
5. Carefully lift dough directly onto grill rack. Brush $^1/_2$ teaspoon of remaining oil over top side of each crust. Grill about 2 minutes, until dough bubbles and begins to char on bottom; turn. Evenly distribute half of the potatoes, onion, olives, arugula and cheese over each crust. Close grill cover or tent with foil. Grill 3–5 minutes, until toppings are warm and crust is crisp. Cut into quarters and serve.

Serving (one-half of 8" pie) provides: 1 Fat, 1 $^1/_4$ Vegetables, 2 $^1/_4$ Breads, 25 Optional Calories.

Per serving: 303 Calories, 8 g Total Fat, 1 g Saturated Fat, 2 mg Cholesterol, 562 mg Sodium, 51 g Total Carbohydrate, 4 g Dietary Fiber, 8 g Protein, 71 mg Calcium.

APPLE, RAISIN, FETA CHEESE & CARROT PIZZA

The sweetness of apple, raisins and carrots works beautifully with the tang of feta cheese in this most unusual pizza.

Makes 4 servings

1 tablespoon all-purpose flour
1 recipe Pizza Dough (page 132)
1 teaspoon walnut or vegetable oil
1 ¹/₂ ounces feta cheese, crumbled
3 small apples, cored and thinly sliced

¹/₂ ounce finely chopped walnuts
¹/₄ cup raisins
¹/₂ teaspoon slivered fresh sage
   (or ¹/₄ teaspoon dried)

1. Prepare grill for a hot fire, using direct method (see page xiii).
2. Sprinkle work surface with flour. With rolling pin, roll out dough to two 8" circles, approximately ¹/₈" thick.
3. Carefully lift dough directly onto grill rack. Brush ¹/₂ teaspoon of the oil over top side of each crust. Grill about 2 minutes, until dough bubbles and begins to char on bottom; turn. Evenly distribute half of the cheese, apples, walnuts, raisins and sage over each crust. Close grill cover or tent with foil. Grill 3–5 minutes, until toppings are warm and crust is crisp (feta cheese will not completely melt). Cut into quarters and serve.

Serving (one-half of 8" pie) provides: ³/₄ Fat, 1 ¹/₄ Fruits, ¹/₂ Protein, 2 Breads, 15 Optional Calories.

Per serving: 323 Calories, 8 g Total Fat, 2 g Saturated Fat, 9 mg Cholesterol, 395 mg Sodium, 57 g Total Carbohydrate, 4 g Dietary Fiber, 8 g Protein, 76 mg Calcium.

BLUE CHEESE AND PEAR PIZZA

The contrasting flavors of two beautifully matched toppings make this pizza delicious.

Makes 4 servings

1 tablespoon all-purpose flour
1 recipe Pizza Dough (page 132)
1 teaspoon olive oil

1 1/2 ounces blue cheese, crumbled
1 large pear, thinly sliced

1. Prepare grill for a hot fire, using direct method (see page xiii).
2. Sprinkle work surface with flour. With rolling pin, roll out dough to two 8" circles, approximately 1/8" thick.
3. Carefully lift dough directly onto grill rack. Brush 1/2 teaspoon of the oil over top side of each crust. Grill about 2 minutes, until dough bubbles and begins to char on bottom; turn. Evenly distribute half of the cheese and pear slices over each crust. Close grill cover or tent with foil. Grill 3–5 minutes, until cheese is melted and crust is crisp. Cut into quarters and serve.

Serving (one-half of 8" pie) provides: 1/2 Fat, 1/2 Fruit, 1/2 Protein, 2 Breads, 8 Optional Calories.

Per serving: 282 Calories, 6 g Total Fat, 2 g Saturated Fat, 8 mg Cholesterol, 423 mg Sodium, 49 g Total Carbohydrate, 4 g Dietary Fiber, 8 g Protein, 74 mg Calcium.

HERBED PITA BREAD

Makes 8 servings

$^1/_4$-ounce active dry yeast
   (one packet)
1 cup lukewarm water
   (105–115° F.)
2 $^1/_2$ cups all-purpose or bread flour*
$^1/_2$ cup whole-wheat flour
1 tablespoon olive oil

2 teaspoons salt
1 teaspoon dried (thyme or
   or rosemary leaves, crumbled)
$^1/_2$ teaspoon freshly ground
   black pepper
$^1/_4$ teaspoon granulated sugar

1. In small bowl, sprinkle yeast over water; let stand 5 minutes, until foamy.
2. In large bowl or food processor, combine yeast mixture, all-purpose and whole-wheat flours, oil, salt, herbs, pepper and sugar until dough forms. If using food processor, pulse 1 minute until dough begins to form a ball.
3. If mixing by hand, sprinkle work surface with reserved 1 tablespoon flour. Turn dough out onto prepared work surface and knead 5 minutes.
4. Spray medium bowl with nonstick cooking spray; place dough in bowl. Cover loosely with plastic wrap or damp towel and let rise in a warm draft-free place until dough doubles in volume, about 1 hour.
5. Punch down dough; let stand 10 minutes. Divide into 8 equal pieces, forming each piece into a ball. Cover loosely with plastic wrap or damp towel and let stand 30 minutes.
6. Prepare grill for a medium fire, using direct method (see page xiii).
7. Roll or pat out each ball to slightly less than $^1/_8$" thickness. Cover and let stand 30 minutes.
8. Using spatula, transfer pitas to edges of grill. Grill 3–4 minutes, until puffed with brown spots on bottom. Turn and grill 3–4 minutes more. Remove and wrap at once in foil so that breads stay moist; they will deflate as they cool.

Serving (1 pita) provides: $^1/_4$ Fat, 2 Breads, 5 Optional Calories.

Per serving: 188 Calories, 2 g Total Fat, 0 g Saturated Fat, 0 mg Cholesterol, 552 mg Sodium, 36 g Total Carbohydrate, 2 g Dietary Fiber, 5 g Protein, 20 mg Calcium.

*If mixing by hand (step 3), reserve 1 tablespoon flour.

SKILLET-GRILLED CORNBREAD

You can "bake" this cornbread on the top rack while cooking dinner on the rest of the grill.

Makes 8 servings

1 1/4 cups all-purpose flour
3/4 cup cornmeal
1/4 cup granulated sugar
2 teaspoons baking powder

1 cup skim milk
1 egg
2 tablespoons vegetable oil

1. Prepare grill for a hot fire, using direct method (see page xiii). Spray a 10" cast-iron skillet with nonstick cooking spray.
2. In large bowl, combine flour, cornmeal, sugar and baking powder. Stir in milk, egg and oil; mix until dry ingredients are thoroughly moistened.
3. Pour batter into prepared skillet; place skillet on top rack of grill or at least 10–12" from heat. Close grill cover or tent with foil. Bake about 15 minutes, until golden and toothpick inserted in center comes out clean. Cut into 8 wedges and serve.

Serving (one-eighth of cornbread) provides: 3/4 Fat, 1 1/2 Breads, 50 Optional Calories.

Per serving: 194 Calories, 5 g Total Fat, 1 g Saturated Fat, 27 mg Cholesterol, 147 mg Sodium, 33 g Total Carbohydrate, 1 g Dietary Fiber, 5 g Protein, 112 mg Calcium.

CORN AND RICE SPOONBREAD

This is a slightly different version of the usual all-cornmeal spoonbread. It comes out golden and crisp at the edges and fairly firm in the center. It can be made ahead and reheated, and is wonderful with maple syrup for breakfast.

Makes 8 servings

1 cup cooked long-grain white rice
1/4 cup cornmeal
1 cup plain low-fat yogurt
1 cup evaporated skimmed milk
3/4 teaspoon salt

1/2 teaspoon baking soda
1/4 cup fat-free egg substitute, thawed
1 egg, lightly beaten
1 tablespoon butter, melted

1. Prepare grill for a medium fire, using direct method (see page xiii).
2. In medium bowl, combine rice, cornmeal, yogurt, milk, salt, baking soda, egg substitute, egg and butter in that order, whisking just until blended.
3. Place a 9" cast-iron skillet with lid on outer edge of grill 30 seconds; spray with nonstick cooking spray. Spread rice mixture evenly into pan. Cover skillet and grill 25–35 minutes, until crusty and knife inserted in center comes out clean. Cut into 8 wedges and serve hot.

Serving (one-eighth of spoonbread) provides: 1/4 Milk, 1/4 Protein, 1/2 Bread, 30 Optional Calories.

Per serving: 118 Calories, 3 g Total Fat, 1 g Saturated Fat, 33 mg Cholesterol, 376 mg Sodium, 16 g Total Carbohydrate, 0 g Dietary Fiber, 6 g Protein, 155 mg Calcium.

8

MARINADES, SAUCES AND MAKE-AHEADS

Lemon-Rosemary Marinade • Yogurt-Cilantro Marinade

Sweet and Sour Marinade • Moroccan Herb and Spice Rub • Fresh Herb Pesto

Argentine Green Sauce • Texas Barbecue Sauce • Marsala Barbecue Sauce

Roasted Red Pepper Sauce • Lime-Honey Glaze • Carmelized Ginger Onions

Mango–Red Onion Relish • Chunky Tomatillo Topping

Sweet and Hot Peach Chutney • Olive–Orange Relish • Roasted Garlic

Grilled Red or Sweet White Onions • Grilled Peppers • Grilled Corn

LEMON-ROSEMARY MARINADE

This recipe makes a mere $^1/_3$ cup marinade, but, slight as that may seem, it adds a powerful amount of flavor to white-meat chicken. Use it as a tenderizing marinade, or brush it onto poultry as it grills. One batch is perfect for about 10 ounces of skinless boneless chicken.

Makes 4 servings

$^1/_4$ cup hot water
$^3/_4$ teaspoon dried rosemary
   leaves, crumbled
$^1/_2$ teaspoon grated lemon zest*
2 tablespoons fresh lemon juice

2 teaspoons vegetable oil
1 medium garlic clove, minced
$^1/_8$ teaspoon salt
$^1/_8$ teaspoon freshly ground
   black pepper

In heatproof glass measuring cup, pour hot water over rosemary; let cool. Stir in zest, juice, oil, garlic, salt and pepper. Cover and refrigerate until ready to use, up to 1 week.

Serving (about 1 tablespoon) provides: $^1/_2$ Fat.

Per serving: 24 Calories, 2 g Total Fat, 0 g Saturated Fat, 0 mg Cholesterol, 69 mg Sodium, 1 g Total Carbohydrate, 0 g Dietary Fiber, 0 g Protein, 5 mg Calcium.

The zest of the lemon is the peel without any of the pith (white membrane). To remove zest from lemon, use a zester or vegetable peeler. To grate zest, use a zester or the fine side of a vegetable grater.

YOGURT-CILANTRO MARINADE

This simple marinade tenderizes and flavors chicken and lamb, and it's wonderful with fish. The recipe makes about 1 cup marinade, enough for about 1 pound of grilled fish or poultry.

Makes 4 servings

³/₄ cup plain nonfat yogurt
2 tablespoons minced fresh
  cilantro
2 tablespoons fresh lime juice

1 tablespoon + 1 teaspoon
  vegetable oil
1 teaspoon Dijon-style mustard
1 garlic clove, minced

In medium nonreactive bowl, combine yogurt, cilantro, juice, oil, mustard and garlic. Cover and refrigerate until ready to use, up to 1 day.

Serving (¹/₄ cup) provides: ¹/₄ Milk, 1 Fat.

Per serving: 68 Calories, 5 g Total Fat, 1 g Saturated Fat, 1 mg Cholesterol, 63 mg Sodium, 4 g Total Carbohydrate, 0 g Dietary Fiber, 3 g Protein, 87 mg Calcium.

SWEET AND SOUR MARINADE

Brush this Asian marinade on poultry, pork or vegetables as they grill.

Makes 4 servings

$^1/_2$ cup low-sodium chicken broth	1 tablespoon + 1 teaspoon
3 tablespoons rice wine vinegar	dark molasses
12 medium garlic cloves, minced	1 teaspoon Chinese sesame oil*
2 tablespoons reduced-sodium	$^1/_4$ teaspoon crushed red
soy sauce	pepper flakes

In medium nonreactive bowl, whisk together broth, vinegar, garlic, soy sauce, molasses, oil and pepper flakes. Cover and refrigerate until ready to use, up to 1 day.

Serving ($^1/_4$ cup) provides: $^1/_4$ Fat, 20 Optional Calories.

Per serving: 43 Calories, 1 g Total Fat, 0 g Saturated Fat, 0 mg Cholesterol, 319 mg Sodium, 7 g Total Carbohydrate, 0 g Dietary Fiber, 1 g Protein, 71 mg Calcium.

*Available in most grocery stores, Chinese sesame oil adds an intense sesame flavor integral to this marinade. If you substitute regular sesame oil or vegetable oil, the flavor will be very different.

MOROCCAN HERB AND SPICE RUB

Use this rub on chicken, fish or any meat; it makes enough for about one pound. To use, spread over meat and let marinate one hour, then grill and enjoy all the wonderful flavors of North Africa.

Makes 4 servings

1/4 cup minced fresh parsley
2 tablespoons + 2 teaspoons fresh lemon juice
2 teaspoons paprika
2 teaspoons minced fresh mint leaves

1 teaspoon ground cumin
2 medium garlic cloves, minced
1 teaspoon extra virgin olive oil
1/2 teaspoon salt
1/4 teaspoon ground red pepper

In small nonreactive bowl, combine parsley, juice, paprika, mint, cumin, garlic, oil, salt and pepper; mix well. Cover and refrigerate until ready to use, up to 1 day. Stir before using.

Serving (1 tablespoon) provides: 1/4 Fat.

Per serving: 20 Calories, 1 g Total Fat, 0 g Saturated Fat, 0 mg Cholesterol, 278 mg Sodium, 2 g Total Carbohydrate, 0 g Dietary Fiber, 0 g Protein, 16 mg Calcium.

FRESH HERB PESTO

This low-fat pesto is especially good with grilled chicken. It is also wonderful tossed with hot cooked pasta, or as a seasoning for pasta salad.

Makes 4 servings

³/₄ cup fresh parsley leaves
³/₄ cup fresh basil leaves
1 tablespoon fresh thyme leaves
¹/₂ teaspoon salt
1 garlic clove, quartered
¹/₄ teaspoon freshly ground
  black pepper

1 ounce walnuts
3 tablespoons low-sodium
  chicken broth
1 tablespoon fresh lemon juice
1 teaspoon extra virgin olive oil
¹/₂ ounce freshly grated
  Parmesan cheese

1. In food processor or blender, combine parsley, basil, thyme, salt, garlic and pepper; pulse until very finely chopped. Add walnuts and process until nuts are finely chopped.
2. With motor running, pour in chicken broth; process until mixture is smooth. Add juice, oil and cheese; process again until smooth. Cover and refrigerate until ready to use, up to 2 days.

Serving (2 ¹/₂ tablespoons) provides: ³/₄ Fat, ¹/₄ Protein, 10 Optional Calories.

Per serving: 88 Calories, 7 g Total Fat, 1 g Saturated Fat, 3 mg Cholesterol, 352 mg Sodium, 5 g Total Carbohydrate, 1 g Dietary Fiber, 3 g Protein, 151 mg Calcium.

ARGENTINE GREEN SAUCE

This heavenly sauce is ideal on beef—it's the key ingredient in Gaucho Brisket (page 82). Do not make the sauce more than 6 hours ahead; the flavor will become acrid.

Makes 24 servings (1 ¹/₂ cups)

¹/₂ cup coarsely chopped
   fresh cilantro
¹/₂ cup coarsely chopped fresh
   flat-leaf parsley
¹/₄ cup coarsely chopped scallions
   (include some green parts)
¹/₄ cup red or white wine vinegar

1 tablespoon olive oil
2 medium garlic cloves, peeled
1 or more small jalapeño peppers,
   seeded (wear gloves
   to prevent irritation)
¹/₂ teaspoon salt

In blender or food processor, combine cilantro, parsley, scallions, ¹/₄ cup water, the vinegar, olive oil, garlic, pepper and salt; process until quite smooth. Transfer to serving bowl and let stand, covered, 2–6 hours before using, to blend flavors.

Serving (1 tablespoon) provides: 5 Optional Calories.

Per serving: 7 Calories, 1 g Total Fat, 0 g Saturated Fat, 0 mg Cholesterol, 1 mg Sodium, 0 g Total Carbohydrate, 0 g Dietary Fiber, 0 g Protein, 3 mg Calcium.

TEXAS BARBECUE SAUCE

Tomato purée will yield a smooth sauce; crushed tomatoes, a chunkier one. Serve with chicken, burgers, ribs—anything you can think of!

Makes 8 servings

2 teaspoons vegetable oil
1 cup chopped onions
3 cups canned tomato purée or
   crushed tomatoes
3 tablespoons firmly packed
   dark brown sugar
4 garlic cloves, crushed

1 teaspoon chili powder
1 teaspoon dry mustard
$^1/_2$ teaspoon salt
$^1/_4$ teaspoon ground red pepper
2 tablespoons white wine vinegar
Hot red pepper sauce, to taste

1. Place medium saucepan over medium heat 30 seconds; heat oil 30 seconds more. Add onions and 1 tablespoon water; cook, stirring frequently, 4–5 minutes, until translucent. Add tomato purée, $^1/_2$ cup water, the sugar, garlic, chili powder, mustard, salt and red pepper. Bring to a boil; reduce heat to low and simmer, covered, stirring occasionally, 60 minutes, until thickened.
2. Just before using, stir in vinegar and pepper sauce.

Serving ($^1/_4$ cup + 2 tablespoons) provides: $^1/_4$ Fat, 1 $^3/_4$ Vegetables, 15 Optional Calories.

Per serving: 80 Calories, 1 g Total Fat, 0 g Saturated Fat, 0 mg Cholesterol, 517 mg Sodium, 17 g Total Carbohydrate, 3 g Dietary Fiber, 2 g Protein, 28 mg Calcium.

MARSALA BARBECUE SAUCE

This lovely, aromatic sauce, so delicious on pork dishes like Marsala-Barbecued Spareribs (page 75), also complements veal and turkey nicely. It makes enough for about 1 $^1/_2$ pounds of meat or poultry.

Makes 12 servings (about 2 cups)

1 teaspoon vegetable oil
$^1/_4$ cup minced onion
1 medium garlic clove, minced
1 cup tomato sauce
2 fluid ounces ($^1/_4$ cup) Marsala wine or apple juice

2 tablespoons wine or cider vinegar
2 teaspoons firmly packed dark brown sugar
Hot red pepper sauce, to taste (optional)

Place medium saucepan over medium heat 30 seconds; heat oil 30 seconds more. Add onion and garlic; cook until softened, stirring frequently, about 4 minutes. Add tomato sauce, Marsala, $^1/_4$ cup water, the vinegar, sugar and pepper sauce (if using). Simmer over low heat 10 minutes, stirring occasionally. Cover and refrigerate until ready to use, up to 3 days.

Serving (generous 2 tablespoons, with Marsala wine) provides: $^1/_4$ Vegetable, 15 Optional Calories. With apple juice, subtract 6 Optional Calories.

Per serving (with Marsala wine): 22 Calories, 0 g Total Fat, 0 g Saturated Fat, 0 mg Cholesterol, 124 mg Sodium, 3 g Total Carbohydrate, 0 g Dietary Fiber, 0 g Protein, 5 mg Calcium.

Per serving (with apple juice): 17 Calories, 0 g Total Fat, 0 g Saturated Fat, 0 mg Cholesterol, 124 mg Sodium, 3 g Total Carbohydrate, 0 g Dietary Fiber, 0 g Protein, 5 mg Calcium.

ROASTED RED PEPPER SAUCE

Use this sauce of sweet red peppers on hot pasta, broiled chicken or fish, or grilled summer vegetables.

Makes 4 servings

7 medium red bell peppers
1 tablespoon + 1 teaspoon
   balsamic vinegar
2 teaspoons olive oil

4 medium garlic cloves, minced
$^1/_8$ teaspoon ground red pepper
   or hot red pepper sauce

1. Preheat grill for a medium fire, using direct method (see page xiii).
2. Place bell peppers over very hot coals. Grill, turning as needed, until skin is charred on all sides. Place in a heavy paper bag or large covered bowl; let stand 20 minutes.
3. Working over large bowl, carefully remove charred skin, seeds and stems from peppers. Strain juices into blender or food processor. Dice pepper flesh; add to juices in blender. Pour in $^1/_4$ cup water, the vinegar, oil, garlic and pepper; purée until smooth. Transfer to medium nonreactive bowl; cover and refrigerate until ready to use, up to 1 week.

Serving (about $^1/_2$ cup) provides: $^1/_2$ Fat, 3 $^1/_2$ Vegetables.

Per serving: 67 Calories, 3 g Total Fat, 0 g Saturated Fat, 0 mg Cholesterol, 4 mg Sodium, 11 g Total Carbohydrate, 3 g Dietary Fiber, 2 g Protein, 18 mg Calcium.

LIME-HONEY GLAZE

A little of this glaze, brushed on at the end of grilling, adds a lot of flavor to chicken, fish, scallops or shrimp. This recipe makes about ¹/₄ cup—enough for up to 2 pounds of chicken or fish.

Makes 4 servings

Grated zest of 1 lime*
¹/₄ cup fresh lime juice
2 tablespoons honey

¹/₄ teaspoon coriander seeds, crushed

In small nonreactive bowl, combine zest, juice, honey and coriander. Cover and refrigerate until ready to use, up to 2–3 days.

Serving (1 tablespoon) provides: 30 Optional Calories.

Per serving: 37 Calories, 0 g Total Fat, 0 g Saturated Fat, 0 mg Cholesterol, 1 mg Sodium, 10 g Total Carbohydrate, 0 g Dietary Fiber, 0 g Protein, 4 mg Calcium.

*The zest of the lime is the peel without any of the pith (white membrane). To remove zest from lime, use a zester or vegetable peeler. To grate zest, use a zester or the fine side of a vegetable grater.

CARAMELIZED GINGER ONIONS

This naturally sweet condiment is perfect with grilled fish or chicken—or try it on burgers made with beef, chicken, turkey or fish.

Makes 4 servings

2 teaspoons olive oil
4 cups thinly sliced onions
2 teaspoons slivered pared fresh
   ginger root

$^{1}/_{4}$ teaspoon salt
1 teaspoon cider vinegar

1. Place medium skillet over medium heat 30 seconds; heat oil 30 seconds more. Add onions and $^{1}/_{4}$ cup water; cook, stirring frequently, until just beginning to color, about 12 minutes.
2. Add ginger, salt and $^{1}/_{4}$ cup water. Continue cooking, stirring frequently, until onions are sweet and deep brown, about 30 minutes.
3. Just before using, stir in vinegar.

Serving (3 tablespoons) provides: $^{1}/_{2}$ Fat, 2 Vegetables.

Per serving: 82 Calories, 3 g Total Fat, 0 g Saturated Fat, 0 mg Cholesterol, 140 mg Sodium, 14 g Total Carbohydrate, 3 g Dietary Fiber, 2 g Protein, 33 mg Calcium.

MANGO—RED ONION RELISH

This relish is not only beautiful to look at, it's wonderful to eat. Serve along-side any grilled entrée—it's especially good with Pork Chops with Indian Spices (page 73).

Makes 4 servings

1 large mango, pitted
  and diced (about
  1 1/2 cups)
3/4 cup diced red onions
3/4 cup diced seeded ripe tomato

1 tablespoon + 1 teaspoon minced
  jalapeño or serrano
  chile pepper*
2 teaspoons fresh lime juice
1/4 teaspoon salt

In medium nonreactive bowl, combine mango, onions, tomato, chile pepper, juice and salt; stir well. Let stand at least 1 hour before serving, to blend flavors. Cover and refrigerate until ready to use, up to 2 days.

Serving (1/2 cup) provides: 3/4 Fruit, 3/4 Vegetable.

Per serving: 61 Calories, 0 g Total Fat, 0 g Saturated Fat, 0 mg Cholesterol, 143 mg Sodium, 15 g Total Carbohydrate, 2 g Dietary Fiber, 1 g Protein, 18 mg Calcium.

*Serrano chile peppers are small, pointed chiles with a strong hot flavor. Younger green peppers are hotter than the mature red ones. They can be found in Latino grocery stores and some supermar-kets. To avoid burns or irritations, wear gloves when handling serrano or jalapeño peppers, and wash hands immediately afterward.

CHUNKY TOMATILLO TOPPING

Tomatillos, close cousins of tomatoes, are available in specialty grocery stores or Latino markets. Their fresh herblike taste, when paired with zesty onion, is a traditional southwestern accompaniment to chicken.

Makes 4 servings

8 tomatillos (8 ounces), husked and rinsed
1 1/4 cups chopped onions
1 tablespoon minced fresh cilantro

2 teaspoons minced serrano chile pepper*
2 medium garlic cloves, minced
1/4 teaspoon salt

1. Place tomatillos in medium saucepan; cover with 2" water. Cover and bring to a boil; reduce heat to low and cook 5 minutes, until softened. Rinse in colander under cold running water; coarsely chop.
2. In medium nonreactive bowl, thoroughly combine tomatillos, onions, cilantro, chile pepper, garlic and salt. Cover and refrigerate until ready to use, up to 3 days.

Serving (1/4 cup) provides: 1 1/2 Vegetables.

Per serving: 34 Calories, 0 g Total Fat, 0 g Saturated Fat, 0 mg Cholesterol, 137 mg Sodium, 7 g Total Carbohydrate, 1 g Dietary Fiber, 1 g Protein, 17 mg Calcium.

Serrano chile peppers are small, pointed chiles with a strong hot flavor. Younger green peppers are hotter than mature red ones. They can be found in Latino grocery stores and some supermarkets. To avoid burns or irritations, wear gloves when handling serrano peppers and wash hands immediately afterward.

SWEET AND HOT PEACH CHUTNEY

This rich and flavorful chutney will spice up any grilled meat, but it is particularly nice with pork or chicken.

Makes 4 servings

1 teaspoon extra virgin olive oil
1 cup sliced onions
4 medium garlic cloves, minced
2 cups sliced peaches
$^1/_2$ cup cider vinegar
$^1/_4$ cup firmly packed light or
    dark brown sugar

2 tablespoons raisins
1–2 tablespoons thinly sliced
    seeded jalapeño peppers
    (wear gloves to prevent irritation)
$^1/_8$ teaspoon ground ginger
Pinch ground cloves

1. Place medium nonstick saucepan over medium-high heat 30 seconds; heat oil 30 seconds more. Add onion and cook, stirring constantly, until translucent, 6–8 minutes.
2. Add garlic; cook, stirring, 1 minute. Add peaches, vinegar, sugar, raisins, peppers, ginger and cloves. Bring to a boil, reduce heat and simmer gently, stirring occasionally, 50 minutes. Remove from heat and let cool; cover and refrigerate until ready to use, up to 2 weeks.

Serving (scant $^1/_2$ cup) provides: $^1/_4$ Fat, 1 $^1/_4$ Fruits, $^1/_2$ Vegetable, 45 Optional Calories.

Per serving: 135 Calories, 1 g Total Fat, 0 g Saturated Fat, 0 mg Cholesterol, 8 mg Sodium, 33 g Total Carbohydrate, 2 g Dietary Fiber, 1 g Protein, 32 mg Calcium.

OLIVE—ORANGE RELISH

This wonderful relish has flavors reminiscent of the south of France. It is a perfect accompaniment to grilled chicken or a firm-fleshed fish like swordfish or salmon.

Makes 4 servings

2 cups navel orange sections
12 large kalamata olives,
   pitted and diced

$^1/_4$ cup + 2 tablespoons minced
   fresh parsley
1 tablespoon fresh thyme leaves

In medium nonreactive bowl, combine orange sections, olives, parsley and thyme; stir well. Let stand 1 hour before serving. Cover and refrigerate until ready to use, up to 5 days.

Serving ($^1/_3$ cup) provides: $^1/_2$ Fat, 1 Fruit.

Per serving: 92 Calories, 5 g Total Fat, 1 g Saturated Fat, 0 mg Cholesterol, 469 mg Sodium, 12 g Total Carbohydrate, 2 g Dietary Fiber, 1 g Protein, 60 mg Calcium.

ROASTED GARLIC

Roasted garlic can be used as an alternative to margarine when you're serving crusty French bread, or use it to perk up mashed potatoes or sauces. It's a snap to make, and it will keep for weeks in the refrigerator. If you prefer, you can roast garlic in a 350° F oven, on a baking sheet, for 45 minutes–1 hour.

Makes 4 servings

4 small garlic heads

1. Prepare grill for a medium fire, using direct method (see page xiii).
2. Wrap each garlic head in 4 layers heavy-duty foil.
3. Grill garlic 40–45 minutes, until soft. Remove the foil and let garlic cool slightly. Squeeze roasted garlic pulp out of papery skins into small bowl.

Serving (1 tablespoon) provides: 2 Vegetables.

Per serving: 45 Calories, 0 g Total Fat, 0 g Saturated Fat, 0 mg Cholesterol, 5 mg Sodium, 10 g Total Carbohydrate, 1 g Dietary Fiber, 2 g Protein, 54 mg Calcium.

GRILLED RED OR SWEET WHITE ONIONS

Grilled onions are a welcome addition to any summertime salad, sandwich or burger. Grill some up whenever there is room on the barbecue; they won't go to waste! A grill basket is helpful but not necessary.

Makes 8 servings

6 large red or white onions,
cut into ¹/₂" slices

1. Prepare grill for a medium-low fire, using direct method (see page xiii). Spray grill basket, if using, with nonstick cooking spray.
2. Grill onions 20–25 minutes, turning once, until cooked through.

Serving (¹/₂ cup) provides: 1 Vegetable.

Per serving: 35 Calories, 0 g Total Fat, 0 g Saturated Fat, 0 mg Cholesterol, 9 mg Sodium, 8 g Total Carbohydrate, 1 g Dietary Fiber, 1 g Protein, 24 mg Calcium.

GRILLED PEPPERS

Buy bell peppers in assorted colors when their prices fall (usually mid- to late summer), and grill a big batch to keep on hand for salads, sandwiches and pasta dishes. They will keep up to two weeks in the refrigerator.

Makes 16 servings

4 medium green bell peppers
4 medium red bell peppers
4 medium yellow bell peppers
2 fluid ounces (¹/₄ cup) dry white wine
2 tablespoons + 2 teaspoons fruity olive oil
2 tablespoons minced fresh basil (optional)
4–5 garlic cloves, slivered (optional)
¹/₄ teaspoon salt

1. Prepare grill for a hot fire, using direct method (see page xiii).
2. Grill peppers, turning as needed, until skin is charred on all sides. Place in a heavy paper bag or large covered bowl; let stand 20 minutes.
3. Working over large bowl, carefully remove charred skin, seeds and stems from peppers. Strain juices into another large bowl. Slice peppers into strips; add to juices in bowl. Add wine, oil, basil and garlic, (if using) and salt; toss to coat thoroughly. Serve immediately or pack into nonreactive containers, cover and refrigerate up to 2 weeks.

Serving (¹/₂ cup) provides: ¹/₂ Fat, 1 ¹/₂ Vegetables, 3 Optional Calories.

Per serving: 41 Calories, 2 g Total Fat, 0 g Saturated Fat, 0 mg Cholesterol, 35 mg Sodium, 4 g Total Carbohydrate, 1 g Dietary Fiber, 1 g Protein, 7 mg Calcium.

GRILLED CORN

Corn can be grilled in advance and used for a variety of dishes, including salsas, salads, soups and chowders. Once you remove the kernels from the cob, you can also freeze them.

Makes 8 servings

8 small ears corn (5" long)

1. Prepare grill for a medium fire, using direct method (see page xiii).
2. Gently pull back outer leaves of corn husk without removing leaves completely; remove silk. Smooth leaves back over corn and soak in cold water 10 minutes.
3. Grill corn, covered, all vents open, 15–20 minutes.
4. Peel husk away from corn, trim stem and serve immediately. Or let cool, stand cob on end and cut kernels from cob with a knife.

Serving (1 ear or ¹/₂ cup kernels) provides: 1 Bread.

Per serving: 89 Calories, 1 g Total Fat, 0 g Saturated Fat, 0 mg Cholesterol, 14 mg Sodium, 21 g Total Carbohydrate, 3 g Dietary Fiber, 3 g Protein, 2 mg Calcium.

DESSERTS

Grilled Grapefruit • Grilled Cantaloupe with Orange Drizzle
Grilled Bananas with Ginger Sauce • Grilled Spiced Peaches
Grilled Pineapple • Coal-Roasted Stuffed Apples

GRILLED GRAPEFRUIT

This beautifully colored dessert is a perfect, light ending to an elegant meal.

Makes 4 servings

2 medium grapefruit, peeled
and sectioned

4 fresh mint sprigs

1. Prepare grill for a medium fire, using direct method (see page xiii). Spray grill basket with nonstick cooking spray.
2. Arrange grapefruit sections in single layer in prepared basket; grill 4 minutes per side. Divide evenly among 4 plates, using 6 to 8 sections per portion; garnish with mint sprigs and serve.

Serving (one-fourth of grapefruit sections) provides: 1 Fruit.

Per serving: 37 Calories, 0 g Total Fat, 0 g Saturated Fat, 0 mg Cholesterol, 0 mg Sodium, 9 g Total Carbohydrate, 1 g Dietary Fiber, 1 g Protein, 14 mg Calcium.

GRILLED CANTALOUPE WITH ORANGE DRIZZLE

This delicious dessert doubles as a wonderful side dish with pork or chicken. Just omit the orange juice and liqueur; instead, combine 2 tablespoons fresh lime juice with a pinch each salt and ground red pepper; drizzle over the grilled melon.

Makes 4 servings

1 ripe small cantaloupe, seeded and cut into 1" chunks

2 tablespoons fresh orange juice

1 fluid ounce (2 tablespoons) orange-flavored liqueur

1. Prepare grill for a medium fire, using direct method (see page xiii). If using wooden skewers, soak in water 30 minutes.
2. Thread cantaloupe chunks onto six 12" metal or wooden skewers and place at edge of grill. Grill 3–5 minutes, turning often, until warmed through. Do not char. Remove cantaloupe from skewers and place in serving bowl.
3. In small bowl combine orange juice and liqueur; drizzle over hot cantaloupe and serve.

Serving (one-fourth of cantaloupe, with 1 tablespoon sauce) provides: 1 Fruit, 30 Optional Calories.

Per serving: 64 Calories, 0 g Total Fat, 0 g Saturated Fat, 0 mg Cholesterol, 10 mg Sodium, 13 g Total Carbohydrate, 1 g Dietary Fiber, 1 g Protein, 13 mg Calcium.

GRILLED BANANAS WITH GINGER SAUCE

This is sure to be a favorite. For a special treat, serve with a scoop of nonfat frozen yogurt.

Makes 4 servings

1 tablespoon + 1 teaspoon firmly
    packed brown sugar
2 teaspoons fresh lime juice

$^1/_2$ teaspoon grated pared
    fresh ginger root
2 medium bananas, split lengthwise

1. Prepare grill for a hot fire, using direct method (see page xiii).
2. In small bowl, combine sugar, lime juice and ginger. Set aside.
3. Grill bananas 8–10 minutes, turning once, until browned. Place 1 banana half on each of 4 dessert plates; drizzle each with 1 teaspoon sauce and serve warm.

Serving ($^1/_2$ banana, with 1 teaspoon sauce) provides: 1 Fruit, 15 Optional Calories.

Per serving: 69 Calories, 0 g Total Fat, 0 g Saturated Fat, 0 mg Cholesterol, 2 mg Sodium, 18 g Total Carbohydrate, 1 g Dietary Fiber, 1 g Protein, 7 mg Calcium.

GRILLED SPICED PEACHES

Cook these on the side of the grill while you're grilling an entrée, or in your broiler. Nectarines also work beautifully.

Makes 6 servings

2 tablespoons reduced-calorie unsalted tub margarine, melted
2 teaspoons firmly packed dark brown sugar
$^1/_2$ teaspoon vanilla extract

$^1/_4$ teaspoon cinnamon
$^1/_4$ teaspoon rum extract
Pinch ground allspice
6 medium peaches

1. Prepare grill for a medium fire, using direct method (see page xiii).
2. In small bowl, combine margarine, sugar, vanilla, cinnamon, rum extract and allspice.
3. Slice each peach in half vertically, removing pit. Place peach halves, cut-side up, in a double row in center of a double thickness of foil. With pastry brush, spread cut side of each peach half liberally with margarine mixture, letting some pool in the center of each half. Make packet by bringing 2 sides of foil up to meet in center and pressing edges together in two $^1/_2$" folds. Then fold edges of each end together in two $^1/_2$" folds. Allowing room for packet to expand, crimp edges together to seal.
4. Grill until peaches are soft, 15–20 minutes. Remove from grill and open packet carefully, as hot steam will escape. Place 2 halves on each of 6 dessert plates and serve.

Serving (2 halves) provides: $^1/_2$ Fat, 1 Fruit, 5 Optional Calories.

Per serving: 80 Calories, 2 g Total Fat, 0 g Saturated Fat, 0 mg Cholesterol, 1 mg Sodium, 16 g Total Carbohydrate, 2 g Dietary Fiber, 1 g Protein, 9 mg Calcium.

GRILLED PINEAPPLE

Fresh pineapple, glazed with a touch of maple, rum and cinnamon, then grilled, makes a delicious dessert served warm or at room temperature. It is also a superb condiment with roast chicken or turkey. Store any leftovers in the refrigerator and see how good they taste over breakfast cereal in the morning.

Makes 6 servings

$^1/_2$ cup maple-flavored pancake
  syrup
1 teaspoon cinnamon

$^1/_2$ teaspoon rum extract
1 ripe medium pineapple
  (3 $^1/_2$ pounds)

1. Prepare grill for a medium fire, using direct method (see page xiii).
2. In small bowl, whisk together syrup, cinnamon and rum extract.
3. Pare pineapple, removing crown, skin and eyes; halve lengthwise. Brush halves with syrup mixture and grill, turning frequently and basting often, until glazed and lightly browned, 40–45 minutes.
4. Remove pineapple halves from grill and, with sharp knife, cut away and discard core. Cut each pineapple half into nine $^1/_2$" slices and serve.

Serving (three 2-ounce slices) provides: 1 Fruit, 60 Optional Calories.

Per serving: 139 Calories, 1 g Total Fat, 0 g Saturated Fat, 0 mg Cholesterol, 4 mg Sodium, 35 g Total Carbohydrate, 2 g Dietary Fiber, 1 g Protein, 32 mg Calcium.

COAL-ROASTED STUFFED APPLES

These apples make great little treats at the end of a meal. Roast them in the coals while you're grilling the main course.

Makes 4 servings

1 tablespoon + 1 teaspoon firmly
   packed light or dark brown sugar
1 teaspoon cinnamon
$^1/_4$ teaspoon ground nutmeg
$^1/_4$ teaspoon ground ginger
4 small apples, cored with
   top $^1/_4$" sliced off

$^1/_4$ cup raisins
Four 1-ounce gingersnap cookies,
   crushed into crumbs
2 teaspoons reduced-calorie
   tub margarine

1. Prepare grill for a medium fire, using direct method (see page xiii).
2. In small bowl, combine sugar, cinnamon, nutmeg and ginger; sprinkle $^1/_2$ teaspoon of the mixture inside each cored apple. Gently press 1 tablespoon raisins into each cavity followed by 1 tablespoon gingersnap crumbs; top with $^1/_2$ teaspoon margarine. Sprinkle each with remaining $^3/_4$ teaspoon sugar mixture.
3. Fold an 18" square of heavy-duty foil in half. Place one apple in center of rectangle; fold foil around apple tightly, leaving a long foil "stem" as a handle. Repeat with remaining apples. Nestle apples, "stem"-side up, among coals along the edge of grill. Roast 40–50 minutes. (Or bake in 400° F oven 40–50 minutes.)
4. With tongs, carefully remove apple packets from coals. Cool 3–5 minutes, then carefully peel back foil. Transfer to 4 dessert plates and serve immediately.

Serving (1 apple) provides: $^1/_4$ Fat, 1 $^1/_2$ Fruits, $^1/_4$ Bread, 25 Optional Calories.

Per serving: 146 Calories, 2 g Total Fat, 0 g Saturated Fat, 0 mg Cholesterol, 66 mg Sodium, 33 g Total Carbohydrate, 3 g Dietary Fiber, 1 g Protein, 28 mg Calcium.

METRIC CONVERSIONS

If you are converting the recipes in this book to
metric measurements, use the following chart as a guide.

Volume		Weight		Length		Oven Temperatures	
¹/₄ teaspoon	1 milliliter	1 ounce	30 grams	1 inch	25 millimeters	250°F	120°C
¹/₂ teaspoon	2 milliliters	¹/₄ pound	120 grams	1 inch	2.5 centimeters	275°F	140°C
1 teaspoon	5 milliliters	¹/₂ pound	240 grams			300°F	150°C
1 tablespoon	15 milliliters	³/₄ pound	360 grams			325°F	160°C
2 tablespoons	30 milliliters	1 pound	480 grams			350°F	180°C
3 tablespoons	45 milliliters					375°F	190°C
¹/₄ cup	50 milliliters					400°F	200°C
¹/₃ cup	75 milliliters					425°F	220°C
¹/₂ cup	125 milliliters					450°F	230°C
²/₃ cup	150 milliliters					475°F	250°C
³/₄ cup	175 milliliters					500°F	260°C
1 cup	250 milliliters					525°F	270°C
1 quart	1 liter						

DRY AND LIQUID MEASUREMENT EQUIVALENTS

Teaspoons	Tablespoons	Cups	Fluid Ounces
3 teaspoons	1 tablespoon		¹/₂ fluid ounce
6 teaspoons	2 tablespoons	¹/₈ cup	1 fluid ounce
8 teaspoons	2 tablespoons plus 2 teaspoons	¹/₆ cup	
12 teaspoons	4 tablespoons	¹/₄ cup	2 fluid ounces
15 teaspoons	5 tablespoons	¹/₃ cup minus 1 teaspoon	
16 teaspoons	5 tablespoons plus 1 teaspoon	¹/₃ cup	
18 teaspoons	6 tablespoons	¹/₃ cup plus two teaspoons	3 fluid ounces
24 teaspoons	8 tablespoons	¹/₂ cup	4 fluid ounces
30 teaspoons	10 tablespoons	¹/₂ cup plus 2 tablespoons	5 fluid ounces
32 teaspoons	10 tablespoons plus 2 teaspoons	²/₃ cup	
36 teaspoons	12 tablespoons	³/₄ cup	6 fluid ounces
42 teaspoons	14 tablespoons	1 cup plus 2 tablespoons	7 fluid ounces
45 teaspoons	15 tablespoons	1 cup minus 1 tablespoon	
48 teaspoons	16 tablespoons	1 cup	8 fluid ounces

Note: Measurement of less than ¹/₈ teaspoon is considered a dash or a pinch.

INDEX